Ibn Taymiyya's Cordial Letter of Advice to the Shia

Sheikh al-Islām

Aḥmed ibn ʿAbdilḤalīm

Ibn Taymiyya

Translated by

Abdullah Al-Rabbat

رِسَالَةٌ لَطِيفَةٌ فِي نَصِيحَةِ الشِّيْعَة

لِشَيْخِ الإِسْلَامِ

تَقِيِّ الدِّينِ أَبِي العَبَّاسِ أَحْمَدَ بنِ تَيْمِيَّةَ الحَرَّانِي

رَحِمَهُ اللهُ تَعَالَى

ترجمه إلى الإنجليزية

عبد الله بن محمد فراس الرّبّاط

First Edition, 2023

ISBN: 979-8-218-23345-7

Published by Damask Publishers

Table of Contents

Translator's Preface

In the name of Allah, the Compassionate and Beneficent

I praise Allah, and I ask Him for aid and guidance. I seek refuge in Him from the evils of my soul and the evil of Shayṭān and his minions, and I pray that Allah showers our Prophet with everlasting blessings and salutations. Upon Allah is my reliance, and in Him is my trust. I have no power or ability except through Allah, the Most High, the Great.

When someone is labeled as "controversial" by a large number of people, this often mirrors the limited perspectives and sensibilities of those people, as opposed to being a genuine reflection of that individual's true nature. It is within this context that the messengers and prophets sent by Allah to guide and reform human society were subjected to vilification and defamation by many of those who perceived their initiatives as uncomfortable disruptions and threats to their *status quo.*

This phenomenon was unsurprisingly exhibited in Prophet Muḥammad's ﷺ message to his people, which was also subjected to vicious propaganda campaigns that sought to marginalize him and his early followers. On one occasion, it was reported that the Pagans of Quraysh used to warn people of Prophet Muḥammad, saying, "He has broken our unity and dispersed our authority! His speech is like sorcery that estranges a father from his son, a man from his brother, and a husband from his wife!"[1]

Of course, such propaganda was not only spurious, but it was also ultimately futile. Allah eventually vindicated His beloved messenger, who had simply guided the people to monotheism and virtuous conduct. Eventually, Allah granted His messenger victory over the vile heathens who had persecuted and slandered him, and our prophet rapidly transformed from being the most

(1) Al-Sīra al-Nabawiyya of Ibn Hishām (1/382)

"controversial" man in Arabia at one point to the most beloved and respected man in Arabia.

Like their spiritual and intellectual forebears, the scholars of Islam were subjected to similar waves of propaganda as they sought to preserve Islam and refine it from manmade elements and innovations. These innovations, which gradually infiltrated Muslim societies, often diverted Muslim societies from the faith's core teachings and principles. These incursions occasionally succeeded in forging splinters and sects within Islam, resulting in some heterodox Muslim societies that were opposed to mainstream Islam and scholarship.

Consequently, it is not uncommon to observe mainstream Muslim scholars be subjected to all kinds of slander and propaganda by these nascent heterodox Muslim communities, and such perceptions of Muslim scholars often are more indicative of these communities' destitute spiritual and intellectual state than it is indicative of anything pertinent to the scholars themselves.

Take, for example, this account involving the astute and renowned scholar of Islam, Imām Aḥmed ibn Ḥanbal (d. 241). Al-Sayyārī said: Abū al-ʿAbbās ibn Masrūq al-Ṣūfī informed me, he said: ʿAbdullāh ibn Aḥmed ibn Ḥanbal informed me, he said:

> I was sitting in front of my father one day, and a group of people from al-Karkh (Shi'ites) approached. They began discussing Abū Bakr, ʿUmar ibn al-Khaṭṭāb, and ʿUthmān ibn ʿAffān's caliphates (may Allah be pleased with them), and they spoke excessively. They then discussed ʿAlī ibn Abī Ṭālib's (may Allah be pleased with him) caliphate, and they said even more for a prolonged period of time.
>
> My father then raised his head and said, "You people. You have spoken excessively about ʿAlī ibn Abī Ṭālib and the caliphate. However, the caliphate was not an honor to ʿAlī. Rather, ʿAlī himself was an honor to the caliphate!"

Al-Sayyārī, a transmitter of this account, commented after reporting this story, "I then shared this report with a Shi'ite, and he responded to me, saying, 'You have mitigated half of the hatred in my heart that I once had towards Aḥmed ibn Ḥanbal.'"(1)

قال ابن أبي يعلى في كتاب «طبقات الحنابلة»: أنبأنا يوسف المهرواني، قَالَ: أَخْبَرَنَا عَلِيّ بْن بشران، حَدَّثَنَا أَبُو عُمَر مُحَمَّد بْن عبد الواحد، قَالَ: وأخبرني السياري، قَالَ: أَخْبَرَنِي أَبُو الْعَبَّاس بْن مسروق الصوفي، قَالَ: أَخْبَرَنِي عبد اللَّه بْن أَحْمَد بن حنبل:

قَالَ: كنت بين يدي أبي جالسا ذات يوم، فجاءت طائفة من الكرخيين فذكروا خلافة أبي بكر وخلافة عُمَر بْن الخطاب وخلافة عُثْمَان بْن عَفَّانَ رَضِيَ اللَّهُ عنهم، فأكثروا وذكروا خلافة عَلِيّ بْن أبي طالب رَضِيَ اللَّهُ عنه وزادوا فطالوا. فرفع أبي رأسه إليهم فقال: يا هؤلاء قد أكثرتم القول فِي عَلِيّ والخلافة، عَلَى أن الخلافة لم تزين عليًّا، بل عَلِيّ زينها.

قَالَ: السياري: فحدثت بهذا الحديث بعض الشيعة، فقال: لي قد أخرجت نصف ما كان فِي قلبي عَلَى أَحْمَد بن حنبل من البغض.

This account, if true, is quite telling. One may wonder, "Why did that Shi'ite mentioned in the report's conclusion originally harbor much hatred towards Aḥmed ibn Ḥanbal?" One probable reason is that early Shi'ite partisans fabricated a bundle of traditions that vilified Aḥmed ibn Ḥanbal, falsely portraying him as a hater of ʿAlī ibn Abī Ṭālib.(2) Therefore, when this report presented a contrasting image, highlighting Aḥmed ibn Ḥanbal's genuine reverence of ʿAlī ibn Abī Ṭālib, it considerably mitigated the Shi'ite's original hatred of Aḥmed ibn Ḥanbal.

Many scholars who followed in the footsteps of Aḥmed ibn Ḥanbal and the prophets of yore have been subjected to similar campaigns of disinformation initiated by their theological opponents. It goes without saying that scholars who were known for their unrelenting defense of Islam were more often the targets of such campaigns. Consequently, it is not unusual to find a scholar

---

(1) Ṭabaqāt al-Ḥanābila of Ibn Abī Yaʿlā (1/186)

(2) See, as an example, the two preposterous fabrications reported in ʿIlal al-Sharāʾiʿ of Ibn Bābawayh (p. 457).

known for his love and reverence of ʿAlī and *Ahlulbayt* be widely mischaracterized as a Nāṣibī, an adversary of *Ahlulbayt.* Similarly, it is not uncommon to observe a scholar known for his exceptionally kind conduct be mischaracterized as a vile bigot. Alas, such are the trials endured by God's messengers and their successors, the scholars of Islam.

One of the great scholars who similarly experienced many attempts to distort and misrepresent his legacy was none other than Ibn Taymiyya (d. 728), author of the letter translated in this volume. To many Shi'ites, their knowledge of Ibn Taymiyya is confined to his fervent and scathing critique of Shi'ism, leading to his perception as a notorious and hateful enemy of *Ahlulbayt.* This distorted image is further exacerbated when Shi'ites encounter statements from Ibn Taymiyya taken out of context or misquotations designed to depict him as an enemy of *Ahlulbayt.* However, to the careful and sincere reader, such efforts should prove to be futile, even though the flocks of misinformed sheep are bound to believe and consume such misleading information.

While Ibn Taymiyya's criticisms of Shi'ism stand as superb works in their own right, it is important to note that confining one's understanding of Ibn Taymiyya's life and legacy to a handful of polemical debates and controversies will inevitably result in an incomplete and distorted view of his life and his works.

A comprehensive and meticulous study of Ibn Taymiyya's life will reveal that he was a remarkably amicable person to both friend and foe, regularly exhibiting admirable traits absent in most contemporary partisans and dogmatists. Consider, for example, this incident recorded by Ibn Taymiyya's disciple, Ibn al-Qayyim (d. 751). Ibn al-Qayyim, when discussing the ranks of chivalry (*futuwwa*), specifically the principle of extending kindness to one's enemies or those who cause him/her harm, said:

> I have never seen anyone who embodied these traits more than *Sheikh al-Islām* Ibn Taymiyya (may Allah bless his soul). Some of his senior companions used to say, "I wish I

were to my companions as he was to his enemies and adversaries."

I have never witnessed him utter a prayer against any of them, but he used to utter prayers for them.

On one occasion, I brought him good news of the demise of one of his greatest adversaries, who was most vehement in animosity and harm towards him. He reprimanded me for that and said, "To Allah we belong, and to Him we shall return."

He then immediately rose, made his way to the house of the deceased's family, and offered his condolences at the funeral. He then said to them, "Consider me akin to him in your service. I will assist you in anything whenever you need help," and similar things.

They were elated by that, offered prayers for him, and esteemed his conduct. May Allah bestow His mercy upon him, and may He be pleased with him.[1]

قال ابن القيم في كتاب «مدارج السالكين»: وَمَا رَأَيْتُ أَحَدًا قَطُّ أَجْمَعَ لِهَذِهِ الْخِصَالِ مِنْ شَيْخِ الْإِسْلَامِ ابْنِ تَيْمِيَّةَ - قَدَّسَ اللَّهُ رُوحَهُ. وَكَانَ بَعْضُ أَصْحَابِهِ الْأَكَابِرِ يَقُولُ: وَدِدْتُ أَنِّي لِأَصْحَابِي مِثْلُهُ لِأَعْدَائِهِ وَخُصُومِهِ.

وَمَا رَأَيْتُهُ يَدْعُو عَلَى أَحَدٍ مِنْهُمْ قَطُّ، وَكَانَ يَدْعُو لَهُمْ.

وَجِئْتُ يَوْمًا مُبَشِّرًا لَهُ بِمَوْتِ أَكْبَرِ أَعْدَائِهِ وَأَشَدِّهِمْ عَدَاوَةً وَأَذًى لَهُ. فَنَهَرَنِي وَتَنَكَّرَ لِي وَاسْتَرْجَعَ.

ثُمَّ قَامَ مِنْ فَوْرِهِ إِلَى بَيْتِ أَهْلِهِ فَعَزَّاهُمْ، وَقَالَ: إِنِّي لَكُمْ مَكَانَهُ، وَلَا يَكُونُ لَكُمْ أَمْرٌ تَحْتَاجُونَ فِيهِ إِلَى مُسَاعَدَةٍ إِلَّا وَسَاعَدْتُكُمْ فِيهِ، وَنَحْوَ هَذَا مِنَ الْكَلَامِ.

فَسُرُّوا بِهِ وَدَعَوْا لَهُ. وَعَظَّمُوا هَذِهِ الْحَالَ مِنْهُ. فَرَحِمَهُ اللَّهُ وَرَضِيَ عَنْهُ.

(1) Madārij al-Sālikīn of Ibn al-Qayyim (2/328-329)

A highlight of Ibn Taymiyya's personality is his justice and forgiveness of others, including his own persecutors. Ibn Rajab (d. d. 795) described a shift in power in Egypt with the rise of the Sultan al-Nāṣir, where Ibn Taymiyya's persecutors who were previously in power then became vulnerable and powerless. The Sultan Al-Nāṣir released Ibn Taymiyya from his prison in Alexandria, and he summoned him to a gathering of scholars in Cairo. Ibn Rajab (d. 795) said:

> He (the Sultan) commanded that Ibn Taymiyya be summoned to Cairo honorably in the month of Shawwāl in 709 A.H. The Sultan honored him generously, and he stood up for him and welcomed him in a ceremonial gathering that contained Egyptian and Shāmī judges, the jurists and state officials. He honored him more than them, and he heartened him and consulted with him for a period of time.
>
> It is said that the Sultan consulted with him regarding the judges, and Ibn Taymiyya averted him from that and praised the judges. [And it is said that] Ibn Makhlūf used to say, "We have not seen anyone more chivalrous (*aftā*) than Ibn Taymiyya: we strove to kill him, but when he had authority over us, he forgave us."(1)

قال ابن رجب في «ذيل طبقات الحنابلة»: فلما عاد الْمَلِك الناصر إِلَى السلطنة وتمكن، وأهلك المظفر، وحمل شيخه نصر المنبجي، واشتدت موجدة السلطان عَلَى القضاة لمداخلتهم المظفر، وعزل بَعْضهم: بادر بإحضار الشيخ إِلَى القاهرة مكرما فِي شوال سنة تسع وسبعمائة، وأكرمه السلطان إكراماً زائدا، وقام إِلَيْهِ، وتلقاه فِي مجلس حفل، فِيهِ قضاة المصريين والشاميين، وَالْفُقَهَاء وأعيان الدولة. وزاد فِي إكرامه عَلَيْهِم، وبقي يُساره ويستشيره سويعة، وأثنى عَلَيْهِ بحضورهم ثناء كثيرا، وأصلح بينه وبينهم. ويقال: إنه شاوره فِي أمرهم بِهِ فِي حق

---

(1) Al-Jāmiʿ li-Sīrat Shaykh al-Islām Ibn Taymiyya Khilāl Sabʿatī Qurūn (p. 477-478), Dhayl Ṭabaqāt al-Ḥanābila of Ibn Rajab (4/516-517)

القضاة، فصرفه عَن ذَلِكَ، وأثنى عَلَيْهِم، وأن ابْن مخلوف كَانَ يَقُول: مَا رأينا أفتى من ابْن تيمية، سعينا فِي دمه. فلما قدر عَلَيْنَا عفا عنا.

This forgiving nature of Ibn Taymiyya is a highlight of his persona. Another noteworthy incident involving Ibn Taymiyya and the aforementioned judge, Ibn Makhlūf, was reported by al-ʿUlaymī (d. 928). In that incident, unsubstantial allegations were levelled against Ibn Taymiyya, yet he and his brother were summoned before Ibn Makhlūf and consequently imprisoned for several days. Al-ʿUlaymī (d. 928) said:

> He and his brother, Sharaf al-Dīn, were then imprisoned in the jail for several days. It is said that his brother prayed to Allah and made *duʿāʾ* to Allah against them (their oppressors). However, Ibn Taymiyya prevented him from doing so, and he instructed him, saying, "Rather, say, 'O Allah, grant them a light that will guide them'."(1)

قال العليمي في «المنهج الأحمد»: ثم حُبس هو وأخوه شرف الدين في برج أيّاما. ويقال: إن أخاه شرف الدين ابتهل ودعا الله عليهم، فمنعه الشيخ وقال له: "بل قل: اللّهُمَّ هب لهم نورا يهتدون به."

This is not to deny that Ibn Taymiyya possessed a formidable side to him. Indeed, any sincere Muslim will experience moments where he/she is angered and provoked for the sake of Allah, especially when observing attacks or misrepresentations of the Islamic faith by heretics and disbelievers. In fact, some of Ibn Taymiyya's polemical refutations, such as his *magnum opus* refutation of Shi'ism, *Minhāj al-Sunnah*, understandably are quite scathing and sharp in their style.

A nice insight into Ibn Taymiyya's style therein can be found in the account of the contemporary ex-Twelver cleric who reverted

---

(1) Al-Jāmiʿ li-Sīrat Shaykh al-Islām Ibn Taymiyya Khilāl Sabʿatī Qurūn (p. 606), Al-Manhaj al-Aḥmad fī Tarājim Aṣḥāb al-Imām Aḥmad of al-ʿUlaymī (5/32-33)

to mainstream Islam, Ḥusayn al-Mu'ayyad. He recounted his bumpy journey with Ibn Taymiyya's *Minhāj al-Sunnah*, saying:

> In 1998, a student of mine returned from Ḥajj, and he visited me carrying a book of three volumes. He told me, "I was given this book in Mecca," and he told me that this book contained a very scathing critique of Shi'ism and that a refutation of it must be written.
>
> I took this book. As soon as I began sifting through its contents and chapters and skimming through its discussions, I was shocked. In the Shi'ite seminaries at the time, the Salafi school's critique of Shi'ism was not in circulation whatsoever.
>
> Even the senior clerics of the Shia, when asked about what they knew about *Sheikh al-Islām* Ibn Taymiyya, would not be able to provide an answer indicative of comprehensive knowledge and familiarity. They did not know who *Sheikh al-Islām* was except that he was a scholar of the Sunni Nāṣibīs [...].
>
> I [later] devoted time to *Minhāj al-Sunnah* in study and examination. [...] I would occasionally be provoked by some of Ibn Taymiyya's statements when he was harsh, and I would toss the book aside and not continue reading it. Later, my interest in the thorough verification (*taḥqīq*) found in this book would attract me back to it once again. I would thus return to it, and it was a personal struggle. [...]
>
> Allah willed that this struggle would eventually end with a triumph against the ego. I arrived to a firm conviction that Shi'ism, in its foundations and minutiae, is entirely invalid, and that the Truth was with *Ahl al-Sunnah wa-l-Jamāʿa*, so I submitted to that.(1)

---

(1) Qanāṭ Ṭayba al-Faḍā'iyya. "Majālis al-Ṭayyibīn: Al-Tashayyuʿ al-Khaṭar al-Qādim bi-Ifrīqyā / Sheikh Ḥusayn ʿAbdulQādir Al-Mu'ayyad." *YouTube* video, 26:12. April 8, 2017.

https://www.youtube.com/watch?v=l2lZKN9yPv0

Achieving a balanced understanding of Ibn Taymiyya's personality and methodology is an important precursor to the appreciation of some aspects of his legacy, such as the treatise translated in this volume. This letter authored by Ibn Taymiyya evidently contrasts with *Minhāj al-Sunnah* in its tone and attitude, though both are polemical texts on Shi'ism. That is because both texts were written in different contexts for different audiences.

As stated by Ibn Taymiyya, what prompted him to write this letter was that he encountered a Shi'ite man who possessed a document riddled with historical inaccuracies and teachings that conflicted with some Islamic principles. Ibn Taymiyya then sat with this man and spoke with him about the status and rights of *Ahlulbayt* within the correct Islamic framework, and he then advised him about the errors in found in his document. The man eventually trusted Ibn Taymiyya's counsel and requested a written account of his advice to share with his congregants back home, resulting in this succinct and sweet letter.

Reading this letter, one will quickly recognize that Ibn Taymiyya was quite cordial throughout his discussions and expositions. He commences the letter by establishing a basic common ground between mainstream Islam (otherwise referred to as Sunnism in contemporary settings) and Shi'ism, and he then proceeds to build his argument off that common ground. His amicable and diplomatic approach in this letter are pronounced to the extent that an oblivious reader may initially misconstrue Ibn Taymiyya's stance as an endorsement of Shi'ite beliefs, a far cry from reality!

Nonetheless, this letter is a well-written tract that addresses a multitude of fundamental issues and innovations that persist within Shi'ite communities till this day. While the letter appears to be primarily intended for a Twelver Shi'ite audience, or perhaps a syncretic Sunni-Twelver audience, many of its arguments and insights are equally pertinent to other Shi'ite strands and movements as well.

All in all, I believe this text is a useful primer to understand some of the fundamental problems exhibited in Shi'ism, though it certainly is not a comprehensive refutation of Shi'ism. An impressive feature and utility of this letter is Ibn Taymiyya's relentless ability to deploy Islamic scripture to substantiate and contextualize his arguments. This letter thus serves as a gold mine of Quranic verses and authentic prophetic traditions that relate to the matters addressed by Ibn Taymiyya.(1)

Another valuable resource that I recommend as an introduction to the downfalls of Shi'ite dogma is Al-Mukhlabī's well-written book, *Shi'ism: Between the Lenses of Fact and Fiction.* I suppose reading this letter of Ibn Taymiyya's in conjunction with al-Mukhlabī's book would prove to be a useful and substantive introduction to Shi'ism from an Islamic perspective, and Allah knows best.

---

(1) The majority of prophetic traditions cited by Ibn Taymiyya in this letter are authentic. The few inauthentic traditions cited therein, despite their unreliable isnāds, contain generally sound contents that are substantiated in other texts from the Quran and/or Sunnah.

The Letter

In the name of Allah, the Compassionate and Beneficent

The *Sheikh, Imām*, worshipping scholar (*al-ʿālim al-ʿāmil*), the unmatched of his era (*farīdu ʿaṣrihī*), *Muftī* of the different sects, *Sheikh al-Islām*, Taqī al-Dīn Abū al-ʿAbbās Aḥmed ibn *al-Sheikh al-Imām al-ʿālim* Shihāb al-Dīn ʿAbdilḤālīm ibn *al-Sheikh al-Imām al-ʿAllāma* Majd al-Dīn ʿAbdulSalām ibn Taymiyya (may Allah be pleased with him and may He please him) said:

[Ibn Taymiyya's Preface to His Letter]

This letter is to whomever it reaches from the faithful brothers who ally with Allah and His messenger. "Your ally is but Allah, His messenger and the believers: those who pray diligently and give charity while bowing down. Whoever allies himself with God, His Messenger, and the faithful—surely the Party of Allah is the victorious [Quran 5:55-56];" Those who love Allah and His messenger and acknowledge the rights of the Messenger of Allah's kin decreed by Allah and His Messenger.

It is from one's love and obedience to Allah that he loves and obeys His Messenger, and it is from one's love and obedience to the Messenger of Allah ﷺ that he loves those beloved to the Messenger of Allah ﷺ and obeys those the Messenger of Allah ﷺ instructed us to obey.

As Allah said, "O you who believe! Obey Allah and obey the Messenger, as well as those in authority among you. Should you disagree in anything, defer it to Allah and the Messenger for guidance if you truly believe in Allah and the Last Day. This is better in approach and in consequences. [Quran 4:59]"

رِسَالَةٌ لَطِيفَةٌ فِي نَصِيحَةِ الشِّيْعَةِ

بِسْمِ اللَّهِ الرَّحْمَٰنِ الرَّحِيمِ

قال الشيخ الإمام العالم فريد عصره، مُفتِي الفِرَق، شيخ الإسلام تقي الدين أبو العباس أحمد بن الشيخ الإمام العالم شهاب الدين عبد الحليم بن الشيخ الإمام العلامة مجد الدين عبد السلام ابن تيمية -رضي الله عنه وأرضاه وأعلى درجته:

هذا الكتاب إلى من يصل إليه من الإخوان المؤمنين، الذين يتولَّون الله ورسولَه ﷺ والذين آمنوا .(إِنَّمَا وَلِيُّكُمُ اللَّهُ وَرَسُولُهُ وَالَّذِينَ آمَنُوا الَّذِينَ يُقِيمُونَ الصَّلاةَ وَيُؤْتُونَ الزَّكَاةَ وَهُمْ رَاكِعُونَ وَمَنْ يَتَوَلَّ اللَّهَ وَرَسُولَهُ وَالَّذِينَ آمَنُوا فَإِنَّ حِزْبَ اللَّهِ هُمُ الْغَالِبُونَ)، الذين يحبُّون الله ورسولَه ﷺ ومن أحبَّه الله ورسولُه ﷺ ، ويَعرِفون من حقّ المتصلين برسولِ الله ﷺ ما شرعه الله ورسولُه ﷺ.

فإنَّ من محبَّةِ الله وطاعتِه محبَّةَ رسولِهِ ﷺ وطاعتَه، ومن محبةِ رسوله ﷺ وطاعتِه محبَّة من أحبَّه الرسول وطاعة مَن أمرَ الرسولُ بطاعتِه.

كما قال تعالى: (يَا أَيُّهَا الَّذِينَ آمَنُوا أَطِيعُوا اللَّهَ وَأَطِيعُوا الرَّسُولَ وَأُولِي الْأَمْرِ مِنْكُمْ فَإِنْ تَنَازَعْتُمْ فِي شَيْءٍ فَرُدُّوهُ إِلَى اللَّهِ وَالرَّسُولِ إِنْ كُنْتُمْ تُؤْمِنُونَ بِاللَّهِ وَالْيَوْمِ الْآخِرِ ذَلِكَ خَيْرٌ وَأَحْسَنُ تَأْوِيلاً).

The Prophet ﷺ also said, "He who obeys me has obeyed Allah, and he who obeys my appointed officer has obeyed me. He who defies me has defied Allah, and he who defies my appointed officer has defied me."(1)

The Prophet ﷺ also said, as was reported by the Commander of the Faithful, ʿAlī ibn Abī Ṭālib, (may Allah be pleased with him), "Obedience is only in goodness."(2) And the Prophet ﷺ said, "There is no obedience to any creation if it involves disobedience to the Creator."(3)

May the peace, mercy and blessings of Allah be upon you. I praise to you Allah, the One with Whom there is no deity worthy of worship. He is worthy of praise, and He is capable of everything. And I invoke the blessings of Allah upon the *Imām* of the righteous, the seal of the prophets, Muḥammad ﷺ, Allah's slave and messenger, with many salutations.

Without further ado, Allah (glorified and exalted is He) dispatched Muḥammad ﷺ with the Book and the Wisdom "to guide humanity from darkness into light, with the permission of their Lord, to the path of the Almighty, the Praiseworthy. [Quran 14:1]"

Allah said, "Allah has bestowed blessings upon the believers, as He sent a messenger from their own ranks who recites to them His revelations, purifies them, and teaches them the Scripture and Wisdom; although before that they were in a state of evident error. [Quran 3:164]"

And Allah said, "Remember Allah's favor upon you and what He revealed to you of the Book and Wisdom by which He instructs you. [Quran 2:231]"

---

(1) Ṣaḥīḥ al-Bukhārī (9/61), Ṣaḥīḥ Muslim (3/1466)
(2) Ṣaḥīḥ al-Bukhārī (9/63), Ṣaḥīḥ Muslim (3/1469)
(3) Musnad al-Bazzār (5/356), Musnad Aḥmed ibn Ḥanbal (2/333, 6/432)

وقال النبي ﷺ: "من أطاعني فقد أطاع الله، ومن أطاعَ أميري فقد أطاعني، ومن عصاني فقد عصى الله، ومن عصى أميري فقد عصاني."

وقال ﷺ فيما رواه عنه أمير المؤمنين علي بن أبي طالب رضي الله عنه: "إنما الطاعةُ في المعروف." وقال: "لا طاعةَ لمخلوقٍ في معصية الخالق."

سلامٌ عليكم ورحمة الله وبركاتُه، فإنَّا نَحمدُ إليكم الله الذي لا إله إلا هو، وهو للحمد أهلٌ وهو على كل شيء قدير، ونُصلِّي على إمام المتقين وخاتمِ النبيين محمد عبدِه ورسولِه، صلى الله عليه وسلَّم تسليمًا كثيرًا.

أما بعد، فإنَّ الله سبحانه وتعالى بعثَ محمدًا بالكتاب والحكمة، ليُخرِجَ (النَّاسَ مِنَ الظُّلُمَاتِ إِلَى النُّورِ بِإِذْنِ رَبِّهِمْ إِلَىٰ صِرَاطِ الْعَزِيزِ الْحَمِيدِ).

وقال الله تعالى: (لَقَدْ مَنَّ اللَّهُ عَلَى الْمُؤْمِنِينَ إِذْ بَعَثَ فِيهِمْ رَسُولاً مِنْ أَنْفُسِهِمْ يَتْلُو عَلَيْهِمْ آيَاتِهِ وَيُزَكِّيهِمْ وَيُعَلِّمُهُمُ الْكِتَابَ وَالْحِكْمَةَ وَإِنْ كَانُوا مِنْ قَبْلُ لَفِي ضَلالٍ مُبِينٍ).

وقال تعالى: (وَاذْكُرُوا نِعْمَتَ اللَّهِ عَلَيْكُمْ وَمَا أَنْزَلَ عَلَيْكُمْ مِنَ الْكِتَابِ وَالْحِكْمَةِ يَعِظُكُمْ بِهِ).

Allah also addressed His prophet's wives saying, "And remember what is recited in your homes of Allah's verses and Wisdom. [Quran 33:34]"

That which the Messenger of Allah ﷺ would recite in his wives' homes is the Book of Allah and the Wisdom. The Book of Allah refers to the Quran, and the Wisdom refers to the Prophet's spoken words, which are his *Sunnah.* The Muslims must thus learn both.

In the famous ḥadīth reported by al-Tirmidhī and others from the Commander of the Faithful ʿAlī ibn Abī Ṭālib (may Allah be pleased) with him:

> The Prophet ﷺ said, "There shall be a trial (*fitna*)." I said to him, "What is the way out of it, O Messenger of Allah?"
>
> He replied, "The Book of Allah. It contains news of what occurred before your time, knowledge of what will come after, and judgement for that which occurs between you.
>
> It is the Criterion, separating right from wrong, and it is not a joke. It shall crush any oppressor who disregards it, and whoever seeks guidance from other than it will be misguided by Allah.
>
> It is the firm rope of Allah, the wise remembrance, the straight path, one that cannot be swayed by whims or twisted by tongues. It is not dulled by frequent recitation.
>
> Its wonders are endless. Whoever speaks by it speaks the truth, and whoever acts upon it is rewarded. Whoever rules by it rules justly, and whoever calls to it guides to a straight path."(1)

(1) Al-Jāmiʿ al-Kabīr of al-Tirmidhī (5/22)

وقال لأزواج نبيِّه: ﴿وَاذْكُرْنَ مَا يُتْلَى فِي بُيُوتِكُنَّ مِنْ آيَاتِ اللَّهِ وَالْحِكْمَةِ﴾.

والذي كان يتلوه هو ورسوله ﷺ في بيوت أزواجه: كتاب الله والحكمة، فكتاب الله هو القرآن، والحكمة هي ما كان يذكره من كلامه، وهي سنتُه. فعلى المسلمين أن يتعلموا هذا وهذا.

وفي الحديث المشهور الذي رواه الترمذي وغيره عن أمير المؤمنين علي بن أبي طالب رضي الله عنه، عن النبي ﷺ أنه قال: "ستكونُ فتنةٌ"، قلت: فما المَخْرَجُ منها يا رسولَ الله؟

قال: "كتاب الله، فيه نبأُ ما قبلكم، وخبرُ ما بعدَكم، وحُكْمُ ما بينكم. هو الفصل ليس بالهزل، من تَركَه من جَبَّارٍ قَصَمَهُ الله، ومن ابتغى الهُدى في غيرِهِ أضلَّه الله. وهو حبلُ الله المتين، وهو الذكر الحكيم، وهو الصراط المستقيمِ، وهو الذي لا تَزِيغ به الأهواءُ، ولا تَلتَبسُ به الألْسُنُ، ولا يَخْلَقُ على كثرةِ الردِّ ولا تَنقضِيْ عجائبُه. مَنَ قال به صدقَ، ومن عَمِلَ به أُجِرَ، ومن حَكَمَ به عَدَل، ومن دَعَا إليه هُدِي إلى صراطٍ مستقيم."

Allah (exalted is He) declared in His Book, "And hold firmly to the rope of Allah, altogether, and do not be divided. [Quran 3:103]" He also proclaimed in His Book, "Indeed, those who divided their religion and became sects, you have nothing to do with them. [Quran 6:159]"

Allah rebuked those who fragmented and formed factions and sects, and He praised those who united and held fast to Allah's rope, which is His Book, as a single party of the prophets.

As Allah (exalted is He) said, "And indeed, among his partisans was Abraham. [Quran 37:83]" Abraham was the leader of the prophets, as Allah (exalted is He) said, "And when his Lord tested Abraham with certain words and Abraham fulfilled them, Allah said, 'I will make you a leader of mankind.' Abraham said, 'And my descendants?' Allah said, 'My covenant does not span the wrongdoers.' [Quran 2:124]"

And Allah said, "Abraham was indeed a leader, devoted to God, a monotheist, and was not of those who associated others with Allah," until Allah's statement, "Then We revealed to you, [O Muḥammad], 'Follow the religion of Abraham, the Monotheist. He was not among those who associated partners with Allah. [Quran 16:120-123]"

The Messenger of Allah ﷺ used to teach his nation (*Umma*) to recite upon waking, "We have reached the morning upon the true faith of Islam, the word of sincere devotion, the religion of our Prophet Muhammad, and the rite of our father Abraham, a monotheist Muslim who was not among those who associated partners with Allah (*al-mushrikīn*)."(1)

---

(1) Musnad Aḥmed ibn Ḥanbal (24/77-81)

وقال الله تعالى في كتابه: ﴿وَاعْتَصِمُوا بِحَبلِ اللهِ جَميعًا وَلاَ تَفَرَّقُوا﴾، وقال في كتابه: ﴿إِنَّ الَّذِينَ فَرَّقُوا دِينَهُمْ وَكَانُوا شِيَعاً لَسْتَ مِنْهُمْ فِي شَيْءٍ﴾.

فذمَّ الذين تفرقوا فصاروا أحزابًا وشيعا، وحَمِدَ الذين اتفقوا وصاروا جميعًا معتصمين بحبل الله الذي هو كتابه شيعةً واحدةً للأنبياء.

كما قال تعالى: ﴿وَإِنَّ مِنْ شِيعَتِهِ لَإِبْرَاهِيمَ﴾. وإبراهيم هو إمام الأنبياء، كما قال تعالى: ﴿وَإِذِ ابْتَلَى إِبْرَاهِيمَ رَبُّهُ بِكَلِمَاتٍ فَأَتَمَّهُنَّ قَالَ إِنِّي جَاعِلُكَ لِلنَّاسِ إِمَاماً قَالَ وَمِنْ ذُرِّيَّتِي قَالَ لا يَنَالُ عَهْدِي الظَّالِمِينَ﴾.

وقال تعالى: ﴿إِنَّ إِبْرَاهِيمَ كَانَ أُمَّةً قَانِتاً لِلَّهِ حَنِيفاً وَلَمْ يَكُ مِنَ الْمُشْرِكِينَ﴾ إلى أن قال: ﴿ثُمَّ أَوْحَيْنَا إِلَيْكَ أَنِ اتَّبِعْ مِلَّةَ إِبْرَاهِيمَ حَنِيفاً وَمَا كَانَ مِنَ الْمُشْرِكِينَ﴾.

وكان النبي ﷺ يُعلِّم أمتَه أن يقولوا إذا أصبحوا: "أصبحنا على فطرةِ الإسلام وكلمةِ الإخلاص، ودينِ نبينا محمد ﷺ، وملَّةِ أبينا إبراهيم حنيفًا مسلمًا وما كان من المشركين."

The Messenger of Allah ﷺ said, "Indeed, I have been given the Quran and something like it alongside it. Beware! Let not a satiated person reclining on his couch say one day, 'Between you and us is this Quran, so whatever *ḥalāl* we find therein we shall make permissible and whatever *ḥarām* we find therein we shall make impermissible.' Indeed, I have been given the Quran and something similar to it alongside it!"(1)

This ḥadīth is in agreement with the Book of Allah, as Allah has mentioned in the Quran that the Prophet ﷺ recites both the Book and the Wisdom, which was given to him alongside the Quran. Allah instructed in His book that His rope be grasped onto in unison, and He prohibited division and discord. He instructed that we be a united community, not fragmented groups.

Allah said in His Book, "If two groups of believers engage in combat, make peace between them. But if one of them transgresses against the other, then fight against the one that transgresses until it complies with the command of Allah. Once it complies, make peace between them with justice, and be fair. Allah loves those are fair. The believers are but brethren, so make peace between your brethren, and remain conscious of Allah so that you may receive mercy. [Quran 49:9-10]"

Allah thus ordained that believers are brethren, and He enjoined reconciliation between them in the event of any combat or transgression.

The Messenger of Allah ﷺ also said, "The parable of the believers in their mutual kindness, mercy and compassion is that of a single body: if one organ suffers, the rest of the body comes to its aid in fever and insomnia."(2)

---

(1) Musnad Aḥmed ibn Ḥanbal (28/410-411), Ṣaḥīḥ Ibn Ḥibbān (3/7)
(2) Ṣaḥīḥ al-Bukhārī (8/10), Ṣaḥīḥ Muslim (4/1999)

وقال النبي ﷺ: "ألا إني أُوتيتُ الكتابَ ومثلَه معه، فلا أُلْفِيَنَّ رجلاً شبعانَ على أَرِيْكَتِهِ يقول: بيننا وبينكم هذا القرآن، فما وجدنا فيه من حلالٍ حلَّلناه، وما وجدنا فيه من حرامٍ حرَّمناه. إلا إني أُوْتيتُ الكتاب ومثله معه."

فهذا الحديث موافق لكتاب الله، فإن الله ذكر في كتابه أنه ﷺ يتلو الكتاب والحكمة، وهي التي أُوْتِيَها مع الكتاب، وقد أمرَ في كتابه بالاعتصامِ بحبله جميعًا، ونهى عن التفرق والاختلاف، و [أمر] أن نكون شيعة واحدةً لا شِيَعًا متفرقين.

وقال الله تعالى في كتابه: (وَإِنْ طَائِفَتَانِ مِنَ الْمُؤْمِنِينَ اقْتَتَلُوا فَأَصْلِحُوا بَيْنَهُمَا فَإِنْ بَغَتْ إِحْدَاهُمَا عَلَى الْأُخْرَى فَقَاتِلُوا الَّتِي تَبْغِي حَتَّى تَفِيءَ إِلَى أَمْرِ اللَّهِ فَإِنْ فَاءَتْ فَأَصْلِحُوا بَيْنَهُمَا بِالْعَدْلِ وَأَقْسِطُوا إِنَّ اللَّهَ يُحِبُّ الْمُقْسِطِينَ).

فجعلَ المؤمنين إخوةً، وأمرَ بالإصلاحِ بينهم بالعدل مع وجود الاقتتال والبغي.

وقال النبي ﷺ: "مثل المؤمنين في تَوَادِّهم وتراحُمِهم وتعاطُفِهم كمثل الجسد الواحد، إذا اشتكى منه عضوٌ تَدَاعَى له سائرُ الجَسَدِ بالحُمَّى والسَّهَر."

Similarly, he said, "A believer to another believer is like a building, its different parts supporting each other." The Messenger of Allah ﷺ then interlaced his fingers to illustrate this.(1)

These are the foundations of Islam, which are the Book and the Wisdom. It incumbent upon the faithful to hold fast to Allah's rope unitedly.

[Some Rights of *Ahlulbayt*]

It is undoubtable that Allah has decreed within these foundations the sanctity of the Prophet's successors (*khulafāʾ*), his household, the forerunners in faith, and those who followed them in goodness.

Allah (exalted is He) said, "O Prophet! Say to your wives, 'If you desire the life of this world and its adornments, then come, I will provide for you and release you in a gracious manner. But if you desire Allah, His Messenger, and the Abode of the Hereafter, then Allah has prepared for the righteous among you a great reward.' [Quran 33:28-29]"

According to Imām Aḥmed, al-Tirmidhī and others, Um Salama recounted that when this verse was revealed, the Messenger of Allah ﷺ enveloped ʿAlī, Fāṭima, al-Ḥasan and al-Ḥusayn (may Allah be pleased with them) with his cloak and said, "O Allah, these are my household, so cleanse them of impurities and purify them thoroughly."(2)

---

(1) Ṣaḥīḥ al-Bukhārī (1/103), Ṣaḥīḥ Muslim (4/1999)
(2) Musnad Aḥmed ibn Ḥanbal (44/118-119), al-Jāmiʿ al-Kabīr of al-Tirmidhī (6/132)

وقال: "المؤمن للمؤمن كالبُنيانِ يَشُدُّ بعضُه بعضًا"، وشَبَّكَ بين أصابعِه."

فهذه أصولُ الإسلام التي هي الكتاب والحكمة والاعتصام بحبل الله جميعًا، على أهل الإيمانِ الاستمساكُ بها.

ولا ريبَ أنّ الله قد أوجبَ فيها من حُرمةِ خُلفائِه وأهلِ بيتِه والسابقين الأولين والتابعين لهم بإحسانٍ ما أوجبَ.

قال الله تعالى: (يَا أَيُّهَا النَّبِيُّ قُلْ لِأَزْوَاجِكَ إِنْ كُنْتُنَّ تُرِدْنَ الْحَيَاةَ الدُّنْيَا وَزِينَتَهَا فَتَعَالَيْنَ أُمَتِّعْكُنَّ وَأُسَرِّحْكُنَّ سَرَاحاً جَمِيلاً وَإِنْ كُنْتُنَّ تُرِدْنَ اللَّهَ وَرَسُولَهُ وَالدَّارَ الْآخِرَةَ فَإِنَّ اللَّهَ أَعَدَّ لِلْمُحْسِنَاتِ مِنْكُنَّ أَجْراً عَظِيماً).

وقد روى الإمام أحمد والترمذي وغيرهما عن أم سلمةَ أن هذه الآيةَ لما نزلتْ أدارَ النبيُّ ﷺ كِسَاءَه على علي وفاطمةَ والحسنِ والحسينِ رضي الله عنهم، فقال: "اللَّهُمَّ هؤلاء أهلُ بيتي، فأَذْهِبْ عنهم الرِّجْسَ وطَهِّرْهم تطهيرًا."

The Prophet's *Sunnah* elucidates the Book of Allah, and it clarifies, guides to, and articulates its teachings. Despite the contextual reference to the Prophet's wives, the Prophet's proclamation, "O Allah, these are my household," emphasizes the elevated status of the individuals mentioned in the ḥadīth within his family circle and that they are more worthy of being described as his household, though the Quran also acknowledges his wives as members of his household. That is because the bonds of kinship are stronger than those of marriage.

The Arabs sometimes use certain expressions to convey the thorough encapsulation of a word's meaning, extending beyond its basic denotation. An example of this can be found in the Prophet's statement, "The destitute one (*miskīn*) is not merely the beggar who is turned away with one or two morsels or dates. Rather, the destitute one (*miskīn*) is one who does not find anything to meet his needs, yet remains discreet enough to be overlooked in charitable assistance, and he refrains from insistently soliciting aid from people."(1)

What this means is that the latter individual referenced in the ḥadīth exemplifies the true essence of destitution, in contrast to the beggar, who does not wholly embody it. The beggar, though still considered a destitute person (*miskīn*), has others who occasionally offer him provisions.

Similarly, expressions such as, "This is the true scholar," "This is the true Muslim," or "This is the true enemy" are employed to highlight an individual who epitomizes a particular attribute, even though there may be others who also possess that quality, albeit to a lesser degree. Analogous to this in ḥadīth is what was reported by Muslim in his *Ṣaḥīḥ* that the Prophet ﷺ was once questioned about the mosque founded upon piety, to which he responded, "It is this mosque of mine," referring to the mosque of Medīna.(2)

---

(1) Ṣaḥīḥ al-Bukhārī (2/124-125), Ṣaḥīḥ Muslim (2/719)
(2) Ṣaḥīḥ Muslim (2/1015)

وسنتُه تُفَسِّر كتابَ الله وتُبيِّنُه، وتَدُلُّ عليه وتُعبِّر عنه، فلما قال: "هؤلاء أهلُ بيتي" – مع أن سياق القرآن يدلُّ على أن الخطابَ مع أزواجه – علمنا أن أزواجَه وإن كُن من أهلِ بيتهِ كما دلَّ عليه القرآن، فهؤلاء أحق بأن يكونوا أهلَ بيته، لأن صلةَ النسب أقوى من صلة الصِّهر.

والعرب تُطلِق هذا البيان للاختصاص بالكمال لا للاختصاص بأصل الحكم، كقول النبي ﷺ: "ليس المسكينُ بالطوَّاف الذي تَرُدُّه اللقمةُ واللقمتانِ، والتمرة والتمرتان، وإنما المسكينُ الذي لا يَجِدُ غِنىً يُغنِيه، ولا يتَفَطَّنُ له فيُتَصَدَّق عليه، ولا يسأل الناسَ إلحافًا."

بيَّن بذلك أن هذا مختصٌّ بكمالِ المسكنة، بخلاف الطوَّاف فإنه لا تَكمُل فيه المسكنةُ، لوجودِ من يُعطِيه أحيانًا، مع أنه مسكينٌ أيضًا.

ويقال: هذا هو العالم، وهذا هو العدوّ، وهذا هو المسلم، لمن كَمُلَ فيه ذلك، وإنْ شاركه غيرُه في ذلك وكان دونَه. ونظيرُ هذا الحديثِ ما رواه مسلم في صحيحه عن النبي ﷺ أنه سُئِل عن المسجد الذي أُسِّسَ على التقوى، فقال: "مسجدي هذا" – يعني مسجد المدينة.

Nonetheless, the context of the Quranic verses about the Mosque of Dissent (*Ḍirār*),(1) which state, "Do not ever stand in it. A mosque founded upon piety from its inception is more deserving of you standing for prayer within in it. In it are men who love to purify themselves, and Allah loves those who purify themselves [Quran 9:108]," entails that the intended mosque is Qubāʾ Mosque.

It is mass-transmitted that the Prophet ﷺ once asked the congregants of Qubāʾ Mosque, "What is this act of purification for which Allah has praised you?" They replied, "We cleanse ourselves with water [following excretion]."(2)

Nonetheless, the Prophet's Mosque is more worthy of the distinction of being founded upon piety than Qubāʾ mosque, though both were established upon piety and though Qubāʾ Mosque is more worthy of the Prophet's prayer within it than the Mosque of Dissent (*al-Ḍirār*).

It is established that the Prophet ﷺ used to visit Qubāʾ Mosque every Saturday, both on foot and on horseback.(3) As such, he would stand in his mosque for the congregational prayer on Fridays and in Qubāʾ Mosque on Saturdays. In both instances, he was standing in a mosque that could be characterized as being founded upon piety.

When Allah (exalted is He) expressed His intent to cleanse the Prophet's household and purify them thoroughly, the Prophet gathered his nearest and dearest relatives: ʿAlī, Fāṭima (may Allah be pleased with them both), and the two leaders of paradise's youth, al-Ḥasan and al-Ḥusayn. In doing so, Allah granted them two things: He ordained their purification, and He ordained its perfection for them through the *duʿāʾ* of the Prophet ﷺ.

---

(1) The Mosque of Dissent (*al-Ḍirār)* was a mosque established by the hypocrites with the intention of facilitating dissent and disbelief. It was addressed in the Quran in the verses referenced by Ibn Taymiyya, and it was consequently demolished by the Messenger of Allah. See Tafsīr al-Ṭabarī (11/672-681).

(2) Ṣaḥīḥ Ibn Khuzayma (1/45), al-Mustadrak ʿalā al-Ṣaḥīḥayn (1/257-258, 1/299)

(3) Ṣaḥīḥ al-Bukhārī (2/60-61), Ṣaḥīḥ Muslim (2/1017)

مع أن سياق القرآن في قوله عن مسجد الضرار: (لا تَقُمْ فِيهِ أَبَداً لَمَسْجِدٌ أُسِّسَ عَلَى التَّقْوَى مِنْ أَوَّلِ يَوْمٍ أَحَقُّ أَنْ تَقُومَ فِيهِ فِيهِ رِجَالٌ يُحِبُّونَ أَنْ يَتَطَهَّرُوا وَاللَّهُ يُحِبُّ الْمُطَّهِّرِينَ) يقتضي أنه مسجد قُباء.

فإنه قد تَواتَر أنه قال لأهل قباء: "ما هذا الطهور الذي أثنى الله عليكم به؟" فقالوا: لأننا نَستنجيْ بالماء.

لكن مسجده أحقُّ بأن يكون مؤسَّسًا على التقوى من مسجد قُباء، وإن كان كلٌّ منهما مؤسّسًا على التقوى، وهو أحقُّ أن يقوم فيه من مسجد الضرار.

فقد ثبتَ عنه ﷺ أنه كان يأتي قُباءَ كلَّ سَبْتٍ راكبًا وماشيًا. فكان يقوم في مسجده القيامَ الجامعَ يومَ الجمعة، ثمَّ يقومُ بقُباءَ يوم السبت، وفي كلٍّ منهما قد قامَ في المسجد المؤسَّسِ على التقوى.

ولمَّا بيَّن سبحانَه أنه يُريد أن يُذْهِب الرجسَ عن أهلِ ببتِه ويُطَهِّرهم تطهيرا، دعا النبيُّ ﷺ لأقربِ أهلِ بيتهِ وأعظمِهم اختصاصًا به، وهم: عليٌّ وفاطمةُ رضي الله عنهما وسيِّدا شباب أهل الجنة، جمع الله لهم بين أن قَضى لهم بالتطهير، وبين أن قضى لهم بكمال دعاء النبي ﷺ.[1]

---

(1) أشكلت علي هذه الجملة، فاستشرت الشيخ نبيل نصار شيخ حفظه الله في معناها، فأجاب بأنّ السياق قد يكون اعتراه تصحيف. ولعل الصواب: "قضى لهم بكماله بدعاء النبي." والله تعالى أعلم.

In that is evidence for us that their purification and cleansing from impurities were a blessing bestowed upon them by Allah. It was a mercy and virtue that He bestowed upon them which they did not achieve through their own efforts and abilities. Otherwise, they would have been able to attain this purification through their inherent virtues without the necessity of the Prophet's prayers, akin to an individual who believes they can thrive by virtue of their own guidance and obedience, independent of Allah's support and direction.

It has also been established by reliable transmission that upon the revelation of these verses, concerning the purification of the Prophet's household, the Messenger of Allah ﷺ recited them to his wives. He then presented them with a choice, as directed by Allah, to either remain his wives or seek divorce. They ultimately opted for Allah, His Messenger, and the abode of the Hereafter.(1) Consequently, the Messenger of Allah ﷺ maintained them as his wives and did not divorce them, remaining married to them until his demise. Had his wives yearned for the material world (*Dunyā*) and its adornments, he would have provided them with compensation and divorced them, as instructed by Allah. Indeed, he was the most reverent of his Lord among the *Ummah* and the most cognizant of Allah's boundaries.

In light of the verse's reference to the amplification of rewards and sins, it has reached us that the *Imām* ʿAlī ibn al-Ḥusayn, the ornament of the worshippers (*Zayn al-ʿĀbidīn*) and the delight of Islam (*Qurrat ʿAyn al-Islām*), said, "I hope that Allah bestows upon the virtuous among us twice the reward, and I fear that the wrongdoer among us incurs twice the sin."(2)

---

(1) Ṣaḥīḥ al-Bukhārī (6/117), Ṣaḥīḥ Muslim (2/1103)

(2) It appears that a scribal error has occurred in this tradition, as this statement was reported from al-Ḥasan ibn al-Ḥasan ibn al-Ḥasan ibn ʿAlī ibn Abī Ṭālib. See Kitāb al-Ṭabaqāt al-Kabīr of Ibn Saʿd (7/314) and Juzʾ Muḥammad ibn ʿĀṣim al-Thaqafī (p. 125).

فكان في ذلك ما دلّنا على أنَّ إذهابَ الرجسِ عنهم وتطهيرَهم نعمةٌ من الله ليُسْبِغَها عليهم، ورحمةٌ من الله وفضلٌ لم يبلغوهما لمجردِ حَوْلهم وقوتهم، إذ لو كان كذلك لاستغنوا بهما عن دعاء النبي ﷺ، كما يَظنّ من يَظُنّ أنه قد استغنى في هدايته وطاعته عن إعانةِ الله تعالى له وهدايتهِ إيّاه.

وقد ثبت أيضًا بالنقل الصحيح أن هذه الآيات لما نزلت قرأها النبي ﷺ على أزواجه وخيَّرهن كما أمره الله، فاخترنَ الله ورسولَه والدار الآخرةَ، ولذلك أقَرَّهنّ ولم يُطلِّقْهن حتى ماتَ عنهن. ولو أردن الحياة الدنيا وزينتها لكان يُمتِّعهن ويُسَرِّحهن كما أمره الله سبحانه وتعالى، فإنه ﷺ أخشى الأمةِ لربه وأعلَمهُم بحدودِه.

ولأجل ما دلّت عليه هذه الآيات من مضاعفة للأجور ورفع الوزر، بلغَنا عن الإمام علي بن الحسين زينِ العابدين وقُرَّةِ عينِ الإسلام أنه قال: "إني لأرجو أن يُعطِيَ الله للمحسن منّا أجرين، وأخاف أن يجعل على المسيء منّا وِزرين."

It has been established in the *Ṣaḥīḥ* of Muslim through the account of Zayd ibn Arqam, who said, "The Messenger of Allah ﷺ once delivered a sermon in an oasis situated between Mecca and Medina called Khum, where he declared, 'And my household. I remind you of Allah concerning my household. I remind you of Allah concerning my household.'" When asked, "Who are his household?" Zayd responded, "Those forbidden from partaking in charity (*ṣadaqa*): the House of ʿAlī, the House of Jaʿfar, the House of ʿAqīl, and the House of al-ʿAbbās." Upon being questioned further, "Are these all from his household?" Zayd affirmed, "Yes."(1)

It has also been established from the Messenger of Allah ﷺ through authentic routes that upon the revelation of the verse, "Allah and His angels give blessings to the Prophet. O you who believe, call for blessings on him, and greet him with a prayer of peace [Quran 33:56]," the companions of the Messenger of Allah ﷺ sought guidance on how to invoke blessings upon him. The Prophet ﷺ instructed them, "Say, 'O Allah, bestow blessings upon Muḥammad and the House of Muḥammad as you had done with Abraham and the House of Abraham. Indeed, you are Praiseworthy and Glorious."(2) Furthermore, in an authentic ḥadīth, the Prophet ﷺ also said, "O Allah, bestow blessings upon Muḥammad, his wives and his progeny."(3)

It is also established that on the occasion when the Prophet's son, al-Ḥasan, picked up a date from the dates of charity (*ṣadaqa*), the Prophet ﷺ admonished him, saying, "*Kikh! Kikh!* Were you not aware that charity is impermissible for us, the House of Muḥammad?!"(4) The Prophet ﷺ also said, "Charity (*ṣadaqa*) is impermissible for Muḥammad and the House of Muḥammad."(5)

---

(1) Ṣaḥīḥ Muslim (4/1873)
(2) Ṣaḥīḥ al-Bukhārī (4/146), Ṣaḥīḥ Muslim (1/305)
(3) Ṣaḥīḥ al-Bukhārī (4/146, 8/77), Ṣaḥīḥ Muslim (1/306)
(4) Ṣaḥīḥ al-Bukhārī (2/127), Ṣaḥīḥ Muslim (2/751)
(5) Ṣaḥīḥ Muslim (2/754)

وثبت في صحيح مسلم عن زيد بن أرقم أنه قال: خطبنا رسولُ الله ﷺ بغَدِيرٍ يُدعَى خُم بين مكة والمدينة، فقال: "وأهل بيتي، أُذكِّرُكم اللهَ في أهل بيتي، أذكِّركم اللهَ في أهل بيتي." قيل لزيد بن أرقم: "ومن أهلُ بيته؟" قال: "الذين حُرِمُوا الصدقةَ: آل علي، وآل جعفر، وآل عقيل، وآل عباس." قيل لزيد: "أكلُّ هؤلاء أهل بيته؟" قال: "نعم."

وقد ثبت عن النبي ﷺ من وجوهٍ صحاحٍ أن الله لما أنزل عليه (إِنَّ اللَّهَ وَمَلائِكَتَهُ يُصَلُّونَ عَلَى النَّبِيِّ يَا أَيُّهَا الَّذِينَ آمَنُوا صَلُّوا عَلَيْهِ وَسَلِّمُوا تَسْلِيماً)، سأل الصحابة كيف يُصلُّون عليه، فقال: "قولوا: اللّٰهُمَّ صلِّ على محمد وعلى آل محمد كما صليتَ على إبراهيم وعلى آل إبراهيم، إنك حميد مجيد، وبارك على محمد كما باركتَ على إبراهيم وعلى آل إبراهيم، إنك حميد مجيد." وفي حديثٍ صحيح: "اللّٰهُمَّ صلِّ على محمدٍ وأزواجِه وذريته."

وثبتَ عنه أن ابنه الحسن لما تناول تمرةً من تمر الصدقة قال له: "كخ! كخ! أما علمتَ أنَّا آلَ بيتٍ لا تَحِلُّ لنا الصدقةُ؟" وقال: "إنَّ الصدقةَ لا تَحِل لمحمدٍ ولا لآل محمد."

This ruling – and Allah knows best – is a part of the purification that Allah had ordained for them. Since charity money is considered the people's impurities, Allah purified them of the impurities. Instead, He provided for them from the fifth of the spoils of war (*al-khumus*) and from the *fay'*,[1] which served as a source of sustenance for Muḥammad's household.

As was reported by Aḥmed and others, the Prophet ﷺ said, "I was sent by the sword before the Hour so that Allah be worshipped alone without any partners. My sustenance was ordained under the shade of my spear. Humiliation and disgrace are upon whomever goes against my command. Whoever emulates a people is one of them."[2]

For this reason, it is crucial that people put special care to provide for *Ahlulbayt*, who were prohibited from the consumption of charity, even more than their care for providing for others from the charity. This is especially the case if *Ahlulbayt* cannot access their rightful share from the fifth of the spoils of war (*al-khumus*) or the *fay'*, either due to scarcity or due to the transgression of oppressive rulers who deny them it.

In such circumstances, the *Ahlulbayt* should be given provision from the obligatory *ṣadaqa* to meet their needs if they cannot be sustained through their rightful share from fifth of the spoils (*al-khumus*) and the *fay'*.

(1) *Fay'* refers to wealth that is rightfully acquired from the disbelievers without combat. It spans *jizya*, the fees imposed upon disbelievers for engaging in trade in Muslim lands, the wealth acquired from one who died without any viable inheritors, and the spoils acquired from enemies who flee prior to combat, abandoning their wealth and belongings. See al-Rawḍ al-Murbiʿ Sharḥu Zād al-Mustaqniʿ of al-Buhūtī (p. 375).

(2) Musnad Aḥmed ibn Ḥanbal (9/123)

وهذا - والله أعلم - من التطهير الذي شرعه الله لهم، فإن الصدقةَ أوساخ الناس، فطهَّرهم الله من الأوساخ، وعوَّضَهم بما يُقِيْتُهم من خُمسِ الغنائم ومن الفَيء الذي جُعِلَ منه رِزقُ محمدٍ.

حيث قال ﷺ فيما رواه أحمد وغيره: "بعِثتُ بالسيف بين يَدَي الساعةِ حتى يُعبَد الله وحده لا شريكَ له، وجُعِلَ رِزْقي تحتَ ظِلِّ رُمْحِي، وجُعِلَ الذلَّةُ والصَّغَارُ على من خالفَ أمري، ومن تَشبَّه بقومٍ فهو منهم."

ولهذا ينبغي أن يكون اهتمامُهم بكفايةِ أهل البيت الذين حُرِّمتْ عليهم الصدقةُ أكثر من اهتمامهم بكفاية الآخرين من الصدقة، لاسيَّما إذا تعذَّر أخذُهم من الخمس والفيء، إمّا لقلَّةِ ذلك وإمّا لظلمِ من يَستولي على حقوقِهم فيَمنعُهم إيّاها من وُلاةِ الظلم.

فيُعْطَون من الصدقةِ المفروضةِ ما يكفيهم إذا لم تَحصُل كفايتُهم من الخمس والفيء.

[The Correct Approach to the Companions' Legacies]

Those who receive from the *fay*ʾ, such as the Prophet's kin and others, must embody the qualities outlined by Allah for the recipients of the *fay*ʾ in His Book, where He states, "Whatever Allah restored to His Messenger from the inhabitants of the villages belongs to God, and to the Messenger, and to the relatives, and to the orphans, and to the poor, and to the wayfarer [Quran 59:7]," and the following verses [Quran 59:8-10].

Allah thus divided the recipients of the *fay*ʾ into three categories: (1) the Muhājirīn, (2) the Anṣār, and (3) and those who come after them who pray, saying, "Our Lord, forgive us, and our brethren who preceded us in faith, and leave no malice in our hearts towards those who believe. Our Lord, You are Clement and Merciful. [Quran 59:10]" (1)

This is because the *fay*ʾ merely was acquired through the *jihād*, faith, migration, and support of the Muhājirīn and the Anṣār. Subsequent Muslims merely receive from the *fay*ʾ as part of their legacy left behind, similar to how an heir inherits from his father. If the heir does not share his father's faith, then he is not entitled to inheritance, for a Muslim does not inherit from a disbeliever.(2)

Therefore, anyone who does not pray for the forgiveness of the Muhājirīn and the Anṣār and harbors resentment towards them has disembodied the qualities that Allah has ordained for the recipients of the *fay*ʾ. That is, until his/her heart is sound towards them and until his/her tongue prays for them.

If one of the Muhājirīn or the Anṣār were to hypothetically commit a confirmed sin, Allah would forgive it by virtue of their great good deeds, or through their repentance, or by means of an affliction that expiates their sins, or by allowing the intercession of His Prophet and the believers, or they make *duʿā*ʾ that Allah consequently answers.

---

(1) These categories are mentioned in the Quran 59:8-10.
(2) Ṣaḥīḥ al-Bukhārī (8/156), Ṣaḥīḥ Muslim (3/1233)

وعلى الآخذين من الفيء من ذوي القربى وغيرهم أن يتصفوا بما وصف الله به أهل الفيء في كتابه، حيث قال: (مَا أَفَاءَ اللَّهُ عَلَى رَسُولِهِ مِنْ أَهْلِ الْقُرَى فَلِلَّهِ وَلِلرَّسُولِ وَلِذِي الْقُرْبَى وَالْيَتَامَى وَالْمَسَاكِينِ وَابْنِ السَّبِيلِ) الآيات.

فجعل أهل الفيء ثلاثة أصناف: المهاجرين، والأنصار، (وَالَّذِينَ جَاءُوا مِنْ بَعْدِهِمْ يَقُولُونَ رَبَّنَا اغْفِرْ لَنَا وَلِإِخْوَانِنَا الَّذِينَ سَبَقُونَا بِالْأِيمَانِ وَلا تَجْعَلْ فِي قُلُوبِنَا غِلاً لِلَّذِينَ آمَنُوا رَبَّنَا إِنَّكَ رَؤُوفٌ رَحِيمٌ).

وذلك أن الفيء إنما حصلَ بجهادِ المهاجرين والأنصار وإيمانِهم وهجرتهم ونصرتهم، فالمتأخرون إنما يتناولونه مخلفًا عن أولئك، مشبهًا بتناول الوارث ميراث أبيه، فان لم يكن مواليًا له لم يستحق الميراثَ، فلا يَرِثُ المسلمُ الكافرَ.

فمن لم يستغفر لأولئك بل كان مبغضًا لهم خرجَ عن الوصف الذي وصف الله به أهل الفيء، حتى يكونَ قلبه مسلمًا لهم، ولسانُه داعيًا لهم.

ولو فُرِض أنه صَدَرَ من واحدٍ منهم ذنب محقَّقٌ فإنّ الله يغفره له بحسناتِه العظيمة، أو بتوبة تَصدُر منه، أوْ يَبتليه ببلاءٍ يكفِّر به سيئاتِه، أو يَقْبَل فيه شفاعةَ نبيِّه وإخوانِه المؤمنين، أو يدعو اللهَ بدعاءٍ يَستجيبُه له.

It has been established from the Messenger of Allah ﷺ in the authentic collections (*Ṣiḥāḥ*) through the narration of the Commander of the Faithful, ʿAlī ibn Abī Ṭālib, that Ḥāṭib ibn Abī Baltaʿa wrote a letter to the disbelievers of Mecca as the Prophet ﷺ was preparing to invade them during the expedition of the Conquest (*al-Fatḥ*). Ḥāṭib sent the letter with a woman to inform them of the Prophet's plans. The Prophet ﷺ then received revelation about this, so he dispatched ʿAlī and al-Zubayr to retrieve the letter, and they eventually did. The Messenger of Allah ﷺ then confronted Ḥāṭib, saying, "What is this, O Ḥāṭib?" Ḥāṭib replied, "By Allah, O Messenger of Allah, I did not do this out of malice or disbelief. Rather, I was an individual who resided among the Quraysh but was not one of them. Your companions had ties of kinship that they used to defend their families. I wanted to have a favor upon the Quraysh to defend my relatives [there]." At this point, ʿUmar ibn al-Khaṭṭāb said, "O Messenger of Allah, let me strike this hypocrite's neck!" The Messenger of Allah ﷺ replied, "He has witnessed the Battle of Badr, and who knows? Perhaps Allah looked at the people of Badr and said, 'Do as you wish, for I have forgiven you.'"(1)

Subsequently, Allah revealed the verses, "O you who believe! Do not take My enemies and your enemies for supporters, offering them affection… [Quran 60:1]."

It has also been established in Muslim's *Ṣaḥīḥ* that Ḥāṭib's slave once approached the Prophet ﷺ and said, "O Messenger of Allah, by Allah, Ḥāṭib will enter the Hellfire," as Ḥāṭib used to mistreat his slaves. The Prophet ﷺ responded, "You have erred! He witnessed Badr and al-Ḥudaybiya."(2) The Prophet ﷺ also said, "No one who pledged allegiance beneath the tree shall enter the Hellfire."(3)

---

(1) Ṣaḥīḥ al-Bukhārī (4/59), Ṣaḥīḥ Muslim (4/1941)

(2) Ṣaḥīḥ Muslim (4/1942)

(3) This a reference to the pledge of allegiance that was given to the Messenger of Allah at al-Ḥudaybiya beneath the tree. Rumors had spread within the Muslim

وقد ثبتَ عن النبي ﷺ في الصحاح من رواية أمير المؤمنين علي بن أبي طالب رضي الله عنه أن حاطب بن أبي بلتعةَ كاتَبَ كفَّارَ مكة لمّا أراد النبي ﷺ أن يغزوهم غزوةَ الفتح، فبعث إليهم امرأةً معها كتابٌ يُخبِرهم فيه بذلك، فجاء الوحيُ إلى النبي ﷺ بذلك، فبعثَ عليًّا والزبيرَ، فأحضَرا الكتابَ، فقال: "ما هذا يا حاطبُ؟" فقال: "والله يا رسول الله! ما فعلتُ ذلك أذًى ولا كفرًا، ولكن كنتُ امرأ مُلْصَقًا من قريش، ولم أكن من أنفسهم، وكان من معك من أصحابك لهم قرابات يَحمُون بها أهليهم، فأردتُ أن أتخذَ عندهم يدًا أَحْمِي بها قرابتي." فقال عمر بن الخطاب رضي الله عنه: "دَعْني يا رسولَ الله أَضرِبْ عُنُقَ هذا المنافق!" فقال: "إنه شَهِدَ بدرًا، وما يُدرِيك لعلَّ الله قد اطَّلعَ على أهل بدر فقال: اعملوا ما شئتم فقد غفرتُ لكم."

وأنزل الله تعالى في ذلك (يَا أَيُّهَا الَّذِينَ آمَنُوا لا تَتَّخِذُوا عَدُوِّي وَعَدُوَّكُمْ أَوْلِيَاءَ تُلْقُونَ إِلَيْهِمْ بِالْمَوَدَّةِ) الآيات.

وثَبتَ في صحيح مسلمٍ أن غلامَ حاطب هذا جاء إلى النبي ﷺ فقال: "يا رسولَ الله! واللهِ ليدخلَنَّ حاطبٌ النَّارَ." وكان حاطب يُسيءُ إلى مماليكه، فقال النبي ﷺ: "كذبتَ، إنه قد شَهِدَ بدرًا والحديبيةَ." وقال ﷺ: "لا يدخلُ النَّارَ واحدٌ بايعَ تحتَ الشجرة."

camp that the Prophet's emissary to Quraysh, ʿUthmān ibn ʿAffān, had been murdered, so the Messenger of Allah initiated a pledge of allegiance to avenge ʿUthmān until death, and the Prophet's blessed companions obliged him there and then. See al-Sīra al-Nabawiyya of Ibn Hishām (2/315-316).

Ḥāṭib, who had spied on the Messenger of Allah ﷺ during the expedition for the conquest of Mecca, committed a grave sin by revealing the Prophet's plans, which the Messenger of Allah ﷺ had concealed from his enemy and his companions. Additionally, he mistreated his slaves, and according to the prophetic tradition, "One who is bad in his ownership of slaves will not enter Paradise."[1] However, despite these sins, Allah forgave Ḥāṭib and was pleased with him due to his participation in the battles of Badr and al-Ḥudaybiya, for "the good deeds erase the bad deeds. [Quran 11:114]" How, then, should those who are superior to Ḥāṭib and greater in faith, knowledge, migration, and *jihād* be regarded? None of them committed sins like his.

Furthermore, the Commander of the Faithful ʿAlī (may Allah be pleased with him) narrated this ḥadīth during his reign, with his scribe, ʿUbaydullāh ibn Abī Rāfiʿ, transmitting it from him. In the ḥadīth, ʿAlī reported that he and al-Zubayr were sent to retrieve the letter from the woman, and the Messenger of Allah ﷺ testified on behalf of the people of Badr as he had said. ʿAlī shared this, knowing what had later taken place, to avert people's tongues and hearts from saying nothing but good about the people of Badr. None of the companions committed anything close to what Ḥāṭib had done. Rather, they were diligently seeking the truth in the majority of what they had committed.[2]

---

(1) Musnad Aḥmed ibn Ḥanbal (1/191, 1/209)

(2) What Ibn Taymiyya means here is that Ḥāṭib's espionage was among the greatest transgressions ever done unto Prophet Muḥammad from within his own camp, as it could have compromised his entire operation and facilitated a crushing defeat to the Muslims. Nonetheless, the Messenger of Allah consequently excused Ḥāṭib and praised him. All of the later controversies associated with the Prophet's companions are significantly smaller in magnitude than Ḥāṭib's aforementioned sin. Furthermore, many of the later controversies associated with some companions were disputed matters: those who erred among them had diligently believed that they actually were doing what was right, a stark contrast from Ḥāṭib's scenario.

فهذا حاطبٌ قد تجسَّسَ على رسولِ الله ﷺ في غزوة فتح مكة التي كان ﷺ يَكتُمها عن عدوِّه، وكتَمها عن أصحابه، وهذا من الذنوب الشديدة جدًّا. وكان يُسيء إلى مماليكه، وفي الحديث المرفوع: "لن يدخلَ الجنَّةَ سيئُ الملكة." ثم مع هذا لمَّا شَهِدَ بدرًا والحديبيةَ غفرَ الله له ورَضِيَ عنه، فإن الحسنات يُذهبن السيئات. فكيف بالذين هم أفضلُ من حاطبٍ، وأعظمُ إيمانًا وعلمًا وهجرةً وجهادًا، فلم يُذْنِبْ أحدٌ قريبًا من ذنوبه؟!

ثم إن أمير المؤمنين عليًّا رضي الله عنه روى هذا الحديثَ في خلافته، ورواه عنه كاتبُه عبيد الله بن أبي رافع، وأخبر فيه أنه هو والزبير ذهبا لطلب الكتاب من المرأة الظعينة، وأن النبي ﷺ شهد لأهل بدرٍ بما شهد، مع علمِ أمير المؤمنين بما جرى، ليَكفَّ القلوب والألسنة عن أن تتكلم فيهم إلا بالحسنى، فلم يأتِ أحدٌ منهم بأشدَّ ما جاءَ به حاطبٌ، بل كانوا في غالِب ما يأتون به مجتهدين.

The Messenger of Allah ﷺ said, "If the judge exercises due diligence (*ijtahad*) in a matter and is correct, he will receive two rewards. If he exercises due diligence (*ijtahad*) but errs, he will receive one reward."(1) This ḥadīth is authentic and well-known.

It is also established that during the Battle of the Confederates (*al-Aḥzāb*) – when the disbelievers were repelled in their rage without gaining any advantage, and Allah commanded His Prophet to march to Banī Qurayẓa – the Prophet ﷺ said, "No one should pray ʿAṣr prayer except at Banī Qurayẓa."

Then, while they were en route to Banī Qurayẓa, the time for prayer arrived. Some of the companions said, "We will only pray at Banī Qurayẓa." Others, however, said, "The Prophet ﷺ did not intend for us to miss the prayer. Rather, he intended that we hasten to them," so they prayed on the way to Banī Qurayẓa. In the end, the Prophet ﷺ did not rebuke either group.(2)

This *Sunnah* of the Prophet ﷺ aligns with what Allah mentioned in His book, where He said, "And David and Solomon, when they presided over the dispute pertaining to the field when some people's sheep strayed into at night; and We were privy to their verdicts. And so We made Solomon understand the case, and to each We granted wisdom and knowledge. [Quran 21:78-79]"

Allah (exalted is He) reveals that He granted one of the two prophets the correct understanding of that ruling for that case, and He praised each of them for the knowledge and wisdom that He had bestowed upon them. Similarly, the forerunners among the Muhājirīn, the Anṣār, and those who followed them in righteousness (Allah is pleased with them, and they are pleased with Him), pursued the Truth with due diligence in their disputes.

---

(1) Ṣaḥīḥ al-Bukhārī (9/108), Ṣaḥīḥ Muslim (3/1342)
(2) Ṣaḥīḥ al-Bukhārī (2/15), Ṣaḥīḥ Muslim (3/1391)

وقد قال النبي ﷺ: "إذا اجتهدَ الحاكم فأصابَ فله أجران، وإذا اجتهدَ فأخطأ فله أجرٌ"، وهذا حديث صحيح مشهور.

وثبتَ عنه أيضا أنه لما كان في غزوة الأحزاب فَرَدَّ الله الأحزابَ بغَيظِهم لم ينالوا خيرا، وأمر نبيَّه بقصد بني قريظة، قال لأصحابه: "لا يُصلِّيَنَّ أحدٌ منكم العصرَ إلا في بني قُريظةَ."

فأدركتهم الصلاة في الطريق، فمنهم قوم قالوا: لا نصليها إلا في بني قريظةَ، ومنهم قومٌ قالوا: لم يُرِدْ منّا تفويتَ الصلاة، إنما أرادَ المسارعةَ فصلَّوا في الطريق. فلم يُعنِّف النبي ﷺ واحدةً من الطائفتين.

وكانت سنة رسولِ الله ﷺ هذه موافقةً لما ذكره الله سبحانه وتعالى في كتابه، حيث قال: (وَدَاوُدَ وَسُلَيْمَانَ إِذْ يَحْكُمَانِ فِي الْحَرْثِ إِذْ نَفَشَتْ فِيهِ غَنَمُ الْقَوْمِ وَكُنَّا لِحُكْمِهِمْ شَاهِدِينَ فَفَهَّمْنَاهَا سُلَيْمَانَ وَكُلّاً آتَيْنَا حُكْماً وَعِلْماً).

فأخبر سبحانه وتعالى أنه خصَّ أحد النبيَّين بفهم الحكم في تلك القضية، وأثنى على كلٍّ منهما بما آتاه الله من العلم والحكم. فهكذا السابقون الأولون من المهاجرين والأنصار والذين اتبعوهم بإحسان – رضي الله عنهم ورضوا عنه – كانوا فيما تنازعوا فيه مجتهدين طالبين للحق.

It has been established from the Messenger of Allah ﷺ that he said, "Whoever among you lives after me will witness much discord, so adhere to my *Sunnah* and the *Sunnah* of the rightly guided caliphs after me. Bite onto it with your molars. Beware of innovated matters, for every *bidʿā* (innovation) is a misguidance."(1)

The Prophet's slave (*mawlā*), Safīna, transmitted from him that he said, "The caliphate (*al-khilāfa*) will last for 30 years. After that, it will become a kingship."(2) The conclusion of those thirty years occurred when the Prophet's grandson, al-Ḥasan ibn ʿAlī, conceded governance to Muʿāwiya.

Muʿāwiya was the first of the kings, and there was kingship and mercy in him, as conveyed in the ḥadīth, "There will be a caliphate of prophethood. Then, there will be kingship and mercy. Then, there will be kingship and tyranny. Then, there will be a biting kingship."(3)

It has been established from the Commander of the Faithful, ʿAlī (may Allah be pleased with him), through various routes that when he fought against the partisans of the Camel (*al-Jamal*), he neither enslaved their progeny, seized their wealth as spoils, killed the injured, pursued the fleeing, nor executed the prisoners.(4) Furthermore, it is established that he prayed a funeral prayer for the deceased on both sides at the Battle of the Camel (*al-Jamal*) and Ṣiffīn, and he said, "They are our brothers who have transgressed against us."(5)

ʿAlī affirmed that his adversaries were neither disbelievers nor hypocrites. In his speech, he followed the Book of Allah and the *Sunnah* of His Prophet, as Allah described them as brothers and considered them believers in their combat and aggression. As Allah said, "If two groups of believers fight each other... [Quran 49:9]."

---

(1) Sunan al-Tirmidhī (4/341), Ṣaḥīḥ Ibn Ḥibbān (4/114)
(2) Musnad Aḥmed ibn Ḥanbal (36/248), Ṣaḥīḥ Ibn Ḥibbān (6/8)
(3) Musnad al-Dārimī (2/1334), Musnad al-Bazzār (4/108)
(4) Muṣannaf ʿAbdirrazzāq (10/23), Muṣannaf Ibn Abī Shayba (18/65)
(5) Muṣannaf Ibn Abī Shayba (21/368, 21/392, 21/410)

وقد ثبت عن النبي ﷺ أنه قال: "من يَعِشْ منكم بعدي فسَيرى اختلافًا كثيرًا، فعليكم بسنتي وسنة الخلفاء الراشدين المهديين من بعدي، عَضُّوا عليها بالنواجذ، وإياكم ومُحدَثاتِ الأمور، فإن كل بدعة ضلالة."

وروى عنه مولاه سَفِيْنَةُ أنه قال: "الخلافة ثلاثون سنة، ثمّ تصير ملكًا" ، فكان آخر الثلاثين حين سَلَّم سِبْطُ رسولِ الله ﷺ الحسن بن علي رضي الله عنهما الأمرَ إلى معاوية.

وكان معاويةُ أوَّلَ الملوك، وفيه ملكٌ ورحمةٌ، كما رُوِيَ في الحديث: "ستكون خلافةُ نبوةٍ، ثم يكون ملكٌ ورحمة، ثمَّ يكون ملكٌ وجبرية، ثمَّ يكون ملك عَضُوض."

وقد ثبت عن أمير المؤمنين علي رضي الله عنه من وجوهٍ أنه لمّا قاتَلَ أهلَ الجمل لم يَسْبِ لهم ذُرّيّةً، ولم يَغْنَم لهم مالاً، ولا أَجْهَزَ على جَريح، ولا اتبعَ مدبرًا، ولا قَتلَ أسيرًا، وأنه صلَّى على قتلَى الطائفتين بالجمل وصفين، وقال: "إخوانُنا بَغَوا علينا."

وأخبَرَ أنهم ليسوا بكفَّار ولا منافقين، واتَّبعَ فيما قالَه كتابَ الله وسنةَ نبيِّه ﷺ، فإنّ الله سماهم إخوةً وجعلَهم مؤمنين في الاقتتال والبغي، كما ذكر في قوله: (وَإِنْ طَائِفَتَانِ مِنَ الْمُؤْمِنِينَ اقْتَتَلُوا).

It has been established from the Prophet ﷺ in the authentic collections (*Ṣiḥāḥ*) that he said, "A group shall break away at a time of division among the Muslims. The party more worthy of the Truth will kill them."[1]

This splinter group is the people of Ḥarurā'[2] who were slain by the Commander of the Faithful ʿAlī ibn Abī Ṭālib (may Allah be pleased with him) and his companions as they defected from Islam, rebelled against ʿAlī, and considered him and the rest of the Muslims disbelievers, and desanctified their blood and wealth.

It has been established from the Messenger of Allah ﷺ via mass-transmitted (*mutawātira*) routes that he described them and advocated fighting against them. He said, "One of you would belittle his own prayer when compared to theirs, his own fasting when compared with theirs, and his own recitation of the Quran when compared with theirs. They recite the Quran without it passing their throats. They exit Islam as an arrow that pierces through its target. If those who kill them only knew how much reward they would receive per Muḥammad's tongue, they would have abstained from performing further good deeds."[3]

ʿAlī (may Allah be pleased with him) and his companions consequently killed them. The Commander of the Faithful was immensely delighted for eliminating them, and he prostrated in gratitude to Allah upon recognizing their sign, which was a man who had a fold of skin on his hand with hairs on it. Following that, all of the *Ṣaḥāba* agreed on the permissibility of fighting them, and many, such as Ibn ʿUmar, regretted not participating in their battles alongside the Commander of the Faithful.

---

(1) Ṣaḥīḥ Muslim (2/745)

(2) The early Kharijites who splintered from ʿAlī's camp were referred to as Ḥarūrīs due to their residence in a vicinity near Kūfa named Ḥarūrā'. See Kitāb al-Ansāb of al-Samʿānī (4/134)

(3) Ṣaḥīḥ Muslim (2/748), Sunan Abī Dāwūd (7/146). There are many other variants of this ḥadīth.

وثبت عن النبي ﷺ في الصحاح أنه قال: "تَمرقُ مارقةُ على حينِ فُرقةٍ من المسلمين، تَقتُلُهم أولى الطائفتين بالحق."

وهذه المارقة هم أهل حَرُورَاءَ، الذين قتلوا أميرَ المؤمنين علي بن أبي طالب رضي الله عنه وأصحابَه لما مَرَقُوا من الإسلام وخرجوا عليه، فكَفَّرُوه وكَفَّروا سائرَ المسلمين، واستحلُّوا دماءَهم وأموالَهم.

وقد ثبتَ عن النبي ﷺ من طرقٍ متواترةٍ أنه وصفَهم وأمرَ بقتالِهم، فقال: "يَحقِرُ أحدُكم صلاتَه مع صلاتهم، وصيامَه مع صيامِهم، وقرأنه مع قرآنِهم، يَقرءون القرآنَ لا يجاوزُ حناجرَهم، يَمرُقون من الإسلام كما يَمرُق السَّهمُ من الرَّميَّةِ، لو يَعلم الذين يقتلونهم ماهم على لسانِ محمد ﷺ لنَكَلُوا عن العمل."

فقتلَهم علي رضي الله عنه وأصحابُه، وسُرَّ أميرُ المؤمنين بقتلهم سرورًا شديدًا، وسَجَدَ الله شُكْرًا لمّا ظهرَ فيهم علامتُهم، وهو المُخْدَجُ اليدِ الذي على يَدِه مثلُ البَضْعَةِ من اللحم عليها شَعَراتٌ، فاتفقَ جميعُ الصحابة على استحلالِ قتالِهم. ونَدِمَ كثير منهم - كابن عمر وغيرِه - أن لا يكونوا شهدوا قتالَهم مع أمير المؤمنين.

This contrasts with the events at the battles of the Camel and Ṣiffīn, during which the Commander of the Faithful was distressed by the fighting and mourned the outcome. He and his son, al-Ḥasan, would reconsider their position, with al-Ḥasan advising him that his view was to not proceed.(1)

The joy experienced by the Commander of the Faithful and his companions and the regret felt by those absent from the battle, given the mass-transmitted accounts from the Prophet, cannot be compared to the anguish experienced by the best person from the Prophet's household: his beloved, about whom he said, "O Allah, I love him, so love him and whoever loves him."(2) This is true even though the Commander of the Faithful was more worthy of the Truth than his opponents in all of his conflicts.

The casualties for whom ʿAlī prayed and described as "our brothers" cannot be equated with the casualties for whom ʿAlī did not pray. In fact, when ʿAlī was asked, "Who are the people whose 'efforts in this world are misguided, while they assume that they are doing well [Quran 18:104]'?" He replied, "They are the people of Ḥarūrāʾ."(3)

This distinction between the people of Ḥarūrāʾ and the others exercised by the Commander of the Faithful during his reign in both speech and action, in accordance with the Book of Allah and His Prophet's *Sunnah*, is the correct position. It should be indispensable to anyone guided to the right path, although many scholars from both early and later generations fail to recognize this distinction. Instead, they end up treating them all as one, either diminishing the degree of hatred, condemnation, punishment and killing that the Kharijites deserve or exaggerating the degree of hatred, condemnation, punishment and killing other incomparable people deserve.

---

(1) Muṣannaf Ibn Abī Shayba (21/402, 21/404, 21/149)

(2) Ṣaḥīḥ al-Bukhārī (5/26), Ṣaḥīḥ Muslim (4/1882). This is referring to al-Ḥasan ibn ʿAlī ibn Abī Ṭālib.

(3) Tafsīr ʿAbdirrazzāq (2/346, 3/234)

بخلافِ ما جَرى في وقعة الجمل وصفِّين، فإنّ أمير المؤمنين كان متوجعًا لذلك القتال، مُتشكِّيًا مما جَرَى، يَتَراجِعُ هو وابنُه الحسنُ القولَ فيه، ويذكر له الحسنُ أن رأيَه أن لا يفعله.

فلا يستوي ما سَرَّ قلبَ أميرِ المؤمنين وأصحابه وغَبِطَه به مَن لم يَشْهَدْه، مع ما تواتَر عن النبي ﷺ فيه وساءَه وساَءَ قلبَ أفضلِ أهلِ بيتِه حِبِّ النبي ﷺ، الذي قال فيه: "اللَّهُمَّ إني أُحِبُّه، فأَحَبَّ من يُحِبُّه." وإن كان أميرُ المؤمنين هو أولى بالحق ممن قاتلَه في جميع حروبِه.

ولا يستوي القَتلَى الذين صلَّى عليهم وسمَّاهم "إخواننا"، والقتلَى الذين لم يُصَلِّ عليهم، بل قيل له: مَن ﴿الَّذِينَ ضَلَّ سَعْيُهُمْ فِي الْحَيَاةِ الدُّنْيَا وَهُمْ يَحْسَبُونَ أَنَّهُمْ يُحْسِنُونَ صُنْعاً﴾ ؟ فقال: "هم أهلُ حَرُورَاءَ."

فهذا الفرق بين أهل حروراء وبين غيرِهم الذي سمَّاه أميرُ المؤمنين في خلافته بقوله وفعلِه - موافقًا فيه لكتاب الله وسنةِ نبيِّه - هو الصواب الذي لا مَعدِلَ عنه لمن هُدِيَ رُشْدَه، وإن كان كثيرٌ من علماء السلف والخلف لا يهتدون لهذا الفرقان، بل يجعلون السيرةَ في الجميع واحدةً. فإمّا أن يُقصِّروا بالخوارج عمَّا يَستحِقُّونه من البُغْضِ واللَّعنةِ والعقوبةِ والقتلِ، وإمَّا أن يَزِيدوا على غيرِهم ما يَستحقُّونَه من ذلك.

[The Roots of Guidance and Misguidance and Advice to the Sincere Seeker of the Truth]

The root of this error lies in a lack of knowledge and comprehension of Allah's book, His Prophet's established *Sunnah,* and the precedent of the Prophet's rightly guided caliphs.

Otherwise, whoever seeks guidance from Allah, implores His aid, searches for it, pursues the authentic traditions, and contemplates the Book of Allah, His Prophet's *Sunnah,* and the *Sunna* of his caliphs – particularly the life of the guiding and guided Commander of the Faithful, which witnessed events that perplexed many people, leading them astray due to either excessive adoration for ʿAlī or excessive aversion to him. As reported from ʿAlī, where he said, "Two men shall perish in my regard: an extreme lover who extols me for attributes I do not possess, and an excessive hater who slanders me by things from which Allah had absolved me."(1) – [will arrive at that distinction between ʿAlī's different adversaries].

The foundations and framework behind this are in two things: seeking guidance (*hudā*) and avoiding one's whim (*hawā*) to ensure one is neither misled nor mistaken, but rather upright and in pursuit of guidance. Allah (exalted is He) described His Prophet, saying, "By the star as it fades. Your fellow is neither astray nor misguided. Nor does he speak of his own whims. Rather, it is but a revelation revealed unto him. [Quran 53:1-4]" Allah thus described him saying that he was not astray, meaning that he is not ignorant. Allah also described him saying that he has not erred, meaning that he is not a transgressor.

---

(1) Muṣannaf Ibn Abī Shayba (17/137), Musnad Aḥmed ibn Ḥanbal (2/468-469)

وسببُ ذلك قلَّةُ العلم والفهم لكتاب الله وسنةِ رسوله الثابتةِ عنه، وسيرةِ خلفائِه الراشدين المهديين.

وإلاّ فمن استهدى الله واستعانَه بحثَ عن ذلك، وطلبَ الصحيحَ من المنقول، وتدبَّر كتابَ الله وسنةَ نبيِّه وسنةَ خلفائِه، لاسيَّما سيرةَ أمير المؤمنين الهادي المهدي، التي جرى فيها ما اشتبهَ على خلقٍ كثيرٍ فضَلُّو بسبب ذلك، إمَّا غُلُوًّا فيه وإمَّا جَفَاءً عنه، كما رُوِي عنه أنه قال: "يَهلِكُ فِيَّ رجلانِ: محبٌ غَالٍ يُقَرِّظُني بما ليسَ فيَّ، ومُبغِضٌ قَالٍ يَرمِيْني بما نزَّهَني اللهُ منه."

وحدُّ ذلك ومِلاكُ ذلك شيئانِ: طلبُ الهدى ومجانبةُ الهَوَى، حتى لا يكون الإنسان ضالاً وغاويًا، بل مهتديًا راشدًا. قال الله تعالى في حقّ نبيه ﷺ: (وَالنَّجْمِ إِذَا هَوَى مَا ضَلَّ صَاحِبُكُمْ وَمَا غَوَى وَمَا يَنْطِقُ عَنِ الْهَوَى إِنْ هُوَ إِلَّا وَحْيٌ يُوحَى)، فوصفَه بأنه ليس بضال – وهو الجاهل، ولا غاوٍ – وهو الظالم.

The uprightness of a slave lies in recognizing the Truth and acting upon it. One who does not know the Truth is astray, while one who knows it but acts against it, succumbing to personal whims (*hawā*), is misguided (*ghawā*). A person who knows the Truth and acts upon it possesses true power in worship and genuine insight in knowledge. This is the straight path about which Allah instructed us to say in prayer, "Guide us to the straight path. The path of those You have blessed, not of those who incurred wrath, nor of those who are astray. [Quran 1:6-7]"

Those who incurred wrath are the ones who recognized the Truth but did not follow it, such as the Jews. The astray are those who engage in the acts of the heart and limbs without knowledge, such as the Christians.

Allah thus described the Jews as misguided in His words, saying, "I will turn away from My revelations those who are unrightfully boastful on earth. Even if they were to see every sign, they would not believe in it. And if they were to see the path of guidance, they would not adopt it as a path. And if they were to see the path of error, they would adopt it as a path. That is because they denied Our revelations and paid no heed to them. [Quran 7:146]."

Allah also described the state of a scholar who does not act upon his knowledge, saying, "And recite to them the story of the individual whom We had given Our signs, yet he severed himself from them. Satan thus went after him, and he became among those led astray. Had We willed, We could have uplifted him by those signs; however, he himself clung down to the ground and succumbed to his whims. [Quran 7:175-176]"

And Allah described the Christians as astray, where He said, "And do not follow the whims of a people who had previously went astray, misled many, and deviated from the balanced way. [Quran 5:77]"

فإن صلاحَ العبد في أن يعلمِ الحقَّ ويَعمَلَ به، فمن لم يَعلمِ الحقَّ فهو ضالٌّ عنه، ومَن عَلِمَه فخالفَه واتبعَ هَواه فهو غاوٍ، ومَن علمه وعَمِل به كان من أولي الأيدي عملاً ومن أولي الأبصار علمًا. وهو الصراط المستقيم الذي أمرنا الله سبحانه في كلِ صلاة أن نقول: (اهْدِنَا الصِّرَاطَ الْمُسْتَقِيمَ صِرَاطَ الَّذِينَ أَنْعَمْتَ عَلَيْهِمْ غَيْرِ الْمَغْضُوبِ عَلَيْهِمْ وَلا الضَّالِّينَ).

فالمغضوب عليهم: الذين يعرفون الحق ولا يتبعونه كاليهود. والضالّون: الذين يعملون أعمالَ القلوب والجوارح بلا علمٍ كالنصارى.

ولهذا وصف الله اليهود بالغواية في قوله تعالى: (سَأَصْرِفُ عَنْ آيَاتِيَ الَّذِينَ يَتَكَبَّرُونَ فِي الْأَرْضِ بِغَيْرِ الْحَقِّ وَإِنْ يَرَوْا كُلَّ آيَةٍ لا يُؤْمِنُوا بِهَا وَإِنْ يَرَوْا سَبِيلَ الرُّشْدِ لا يَتَّخِذُوهُ سَبِيلاً وَإِنْ يَرَوْا سَبِيلَ الْغَيِّ يَتَّخِذُوهُ سَبِيلاً ذَلِكَ بِأَنَّهُمْ كَذَّبُوا بِآيَاتِنَا وَكَانُوا عَنْهَا غَافِلِينَ).

ووصف العالم الذي لم يعمل بعلمه بذلك في قوله تعالى: (وَاتْلُ عَلَيْهِمْ نَبَأَ الَّذِي آتَيْنَاهُ آيَاتِنَا فَانْسَلَخَ مِنْهَا فَأَتْبَعَهُ الشَّيْطَانُ فَكَانَ مِنَ الْغَاوِينَ وَلَوْ شِئْنَا لَرَفَعْنَاهُ بِهَا وَلَكِنَّهُ أَخْلَدَ إِلَى الْأَرْضِ وَاتَّبَعَ هَوَاهُ).

ووصف النصارى بالضلال في قوله تعالى: (وَلا تَتَّبِعُوا أَهْوَاءَ قَوْمٍ قَدْ ضَلُّوا مِنْ قَبْلُ وَأَضَلُّوا كَثِيراً وَضَلُّوا عَنْ سَوَاءِ السَّبِيلِ).

Allah also used that descriptor for those who follow their whims without knowledge. He said, "Many go astray by their own whims without knowledge. Your Lord knows best the transgressors. [Quran 6:119]" Furthermore, Allah said, "And who could be more misguided than one who follows his whims without any guidance from Allah? [Quran 28:50]"

Allah also mentioned that a person who follows His revealed guidance will neither go astray like those who are astray nor will he be disheartened like those who incurred wrath. Hence, He said, "However, should guidance come to you from Me, those who follow My guidance will neither go astray nor suffer. [Quran 20:123]"

Regarding this verse, Ibn ʿAbbās said, "Allah guaranteed that whoever reads the Quran and acts upon it will neither go astray in the *Dunyā* nor suffer in the Hereafter."(1)

It is from the thoroughness of guidance that a person seeking it delves into the Book of Allah, the mass-transmitted teachings of His Prophet's *Sunnah* and the *Sunnah* of the [rightly-guided] caliphs, as well as the traditions passed down by the reliable and meticulous transmitters. He must discern those traditions from the traditions passed down by transmitters with poor retention of ḥadīths or those suspected of lying for whatever motive. A transmitter who conveys dubious information may either be intentionally lying or he may unintentionally do so out of poor retention, forgetfulness or lack of comprehension.

---

(1) Muṣannaf ʿAbdirrazzāq (3/381), Muṣannaf Ibn Abī Shayba (15/446), al-Mustadrak ʿalā al-Ṣaḥīḥayn of al-Ḥākim (2/413).

ووصف بذلك من يتبع هواه بغير علمٍ حيث قال: (وَإِنَّ كَثِيراً لَيُضِلُّونَ بِأَهْوَائِهِمْ بِغَيْرِ عِلْمٍ إِنَّ رَبَّكَ هُوَ أَعْلَمُ بِالْمُعْتَدِينَ). وقال: (وَمَنْ أَضَلُّ مِمَّنِ اتَّبَعَ هَوَاهُ بِغَيْرِ هُدىً مِنَ اللَّهِ).

وأخبر أن من اتبع هداه المنزل فإنه لا يضل كما ضلّ الضالون، ولا يَشقَى كما شَقِيَ المغضوبُ عليهم، فقال: (فَإِمَّا يَأْتِيَنَّكُمْ مِنِّي هُدىً فَمَنِ اتَّبَعَ هُدَايَ فَلا يَضِلُّ وَلا يَشْقَى).

قال ابن عباس: "تكفَّل الله لمن قرأ القرآن وعمل بما فيه إلا يَضِلَّ في الدنيا ولا يَشقَى في الآخرة."

ومن تمام الهداية أن يَنظُر المستهديْ في كتاب الله، وفيما تواتَر من سنةِ نبيه وسنةِ الخلفاء، وما نقلَه الثقاتُ الأثباتُ، ويُميِّزَ بين ذلك وبين ما نقلَه مَن لا يَحفظ الحديثَ، أو يُتَّهَم فيه بكذب لغرضٍ من الأغراض، فإنّ المحدِّثَ بالباطل إمَّا أن يتعمد الكذبَ، أو يَكذِبَ خطأً لسوءِ حفظِه أو نسيانِه أو لقلَّةِ فهمِه وضبطِه.

The seeker of guidance, equipped with this knowledge, should reflect upon it. He should compile the ḥadīths that are harmonious, and he should contemplate the conflicting traditions until he eventually comes to the realization that they actually are harmonious as well, though they may appear to be conflicting; Or until he comes to the realization that some of the ḥadīths are preponderant (*rājiḥ*) and should be followed, while others are non-preponderant (*marjūḥ*) and not actually valid evidences, despite appearing to be so.

As for people's error in this regard, it stems from their inability to distinguish between knowledge derived from scripture and traditions and knowledge that is acquired through mere analogical reasoning and contemplation. (1) Then, when such conjecture and error in knowledge are exacerbated by a person's own whims and desires, he earns for himself a share in Allah's statement, "They follow nothing but assumptions and what the ego desires, even though guidance has come to them from their Lord. [Quran 53:23]"

This is due to humanity's innate ignorance in knowledge and propensity for transgression in deeds. With ignorance, one follows conjecture, and with transgression, one pursues egoistic desires. When Allah sent His messengers and revealed His books for the guidance and direction of mankind, those most steadfast in following the messengers were the ones who most diligently avoided these behaviors.

As Allah said, "Mankind were a single nation, and Allah then sent the prophets with glad tidings and warnings. And He sent with them the Book in truth to judge between people in their disputes. None differed over the scripture except its own recipients, spurred by mutual envy between them after the proofs had come to them. And Allah, by His permission, guided the believers to the truth regarding the matters that were disputed. Allah guides whom He wills to a straight path. [Quran 2:213]"

---

(1) Many heresies originate from faulty logical deductions that are then back-projected onto scripture. Such *ad hoc* appeals to scripture are misleading.

ثمَّ إذا حَصَلَتِ، المعرفةُ بذلك تدبَّر ذلك، وجَمَعَ بين المتفق منه، وتَدبَّر المختلفَ منه حتى يتبيَّنَ له أنه مُتّفق في الحقيقة وإن كان الظاهرُ مختلفًا، أو أن بعضَه راجحٌ يَجِبُ اتباعُه، والآخر مرجوحٌ ليس بدليلٍ في الحقيقة وإن كان في الظاهرِ دليلاً.

أما غَلَطُ الناس فلعدمِ التمييز بين ما يُعقَلِ من النصوصِ والآثار، أو يُعقَل بمجردِ القياس والاعتبار، ثمَّ إذا خالط الظنَّ والغلط في العلم هَوَى النفوس ومُنَاها في العمل صارَ لصاحبِها نصيبٌ من قوله تعالى ﴿إِنْ يَتَّبِعُونَ إِلَّا الظَّنَّ وَمَا تَهْوَى الْأَنْفُسُ وَلَقَدْ جَاءَهُمْ مِنْ رَبِّهِمُ الْهُدَى﴾.

وهذا سبب ما خُلِقَ الإنسانُ عليه من الجهلِ في نوعِ العلم، والظلمِ في نوع العمل، فبجهلهِ يتبع الظن، وبظلمِهِ يتبع ما تَهوَى الأنفسُ. ولمّا بعثَ اللهُ رسلَه وأنزلَ كُتبه لهدى الناسِ وإرشادهم، صارَ أشدُّهم اتباعًا للرسلِ أبعدَهم عن ذلك.

كما قال تعالى: ﴿كَانَ النَّاسُ أُمَّةً وَاحِدَةً فَبَعَثَ اللَّهُ النَّبِيِّينَ مُبَشِّرِينَ وَمُنْذِرِينَ وَأَنْزَلَ مَعَهُمُ الْكِتَابَ بِالْحَقِّ لِيَحْكُمَ بَيْنَ النَّاسِ فِيمَا اخْتَلَفُوا فِيهِ وَمَا اخْتَلَفَ فِيهِ إِلَّا الَّذِينَ أُوتُوهُ مِنْ بَعْدِ مَا جَاءَتْهُمُ الْبَيِّنَاتُ بَغْياً بَيْنَهُمْ فَهَدَى اللَّهُ الَّذِينَ آمَنُوا لِمَا اخْتَلَفُوا فِيهِ مِنَ الْحَقِّ بِإِذْنِهِ وَاللَّهُ يَهْدِي مَنْ يَشَاءُ إِلَى صِرَاطٍ مُسْتَقِيمٍ﴾.

Thus, this description of humanity by Allah is not limited to non-Muslims or a specific sect within the *Ummah*. Rather, non-Muslims merely embody these qualities with respect to the foundations of faith (*īmān*), causing their ignorance and transgression in this regard to result in disbelief and grave failure. Similarly, one who introduces a grave innovation (*bidʿa*) in the foundations of the faith embodies these qualities more severely than one who errs or sins in minute matters, but people are often indulgent in highlighting their own merits and the faults of others.

However, a just scholar only speaks the Truth and follows nothing else. One who adheres to the established traditions from the Prophet, his caliphs, his companions, and the scholars of the Prophet's household – such as ʿAlī ibn al-Ḥusayn Zayn al-ʿĀbidīn, his son *Imām* Abū Jaʿfar Muḥammad ibn ʿAlī al-Bāqir, and his son *Imām* Abū ʿAbdillāh Jaʿfar ibn Muḥammad al-Ṣādiq, who is the *sheikh* of the *Ummah's* scholars: Mālik ibn Anas, al-Thawrī and their contemporaries – will find that all of these traditions are harmonious and in agreement with respect to the foundations of their faith and religious rulings.

The follower of these traditions will realize that they are better and more sufficient than the various doctrines later innovated by subsequent figures, which contradict the teachings espoused by the aforementioned predecessors. These later figures either belong to those who harbor animosity towards the Messenger of Allah's ﷺ household, defraud them of their rights, and cause them harm,(1) or they are among those who exceed the proper bounds in venerating them, fabricate lies in their name, and defraud the forerunners and the obedient of their rights.(2)

---

(1) This is a reference to different sects, such as the Kharijites and their Ibadi heirs, who revile ʿAlī ibn Abī Ṭālib and his party. It also spans the Nāṣibīs who resented ʿAlī ibn Abī Ṭālib and many from the Prophet's household. It includes strands of the scholarship that had a staunch ʿUthmānī bias as well.

(2) This is a reference to several extremist Shi'ite strands, such as the Twelvers, the Ismailis, and the Zaydis. The highlight of these different sects is their exaggerated, albeit conflicting, beliefs about *Ahlulbayt* and their transgression

ولهذا صار ما وصفَ الله به الإنسانَ لا يَخُصُّ غيرَ المسلمين دونَهم، ولا يَخُصُّ طائفة من الأمة، لكن غير المسلمين أصابَهم ذلك في أصولِ الإيمان التي صارَ جهلُهم وظلمُهم فيها كفرانًا وخسرانًا مبينًا. ولذلك من ابتدعَ في أصولِ الدين بدعة جليلةً أصابَه من ذلك أشدُّ ممّا يُصيبُ مَن أخطأَ في أمرٍ دقيقٍ أو أذنبَ فيه، والنفوسُ لَهِجَة بمعرفةِ محاسنِها ومساوئ غيرِها.

وأما العالم العادل فلا يقول إلا الحقَّ، ولا يتّبعُ إلا إيَّاه. ولهذا من يَتَّبع المنقولَ الثابتَ عن النبي ﷺ وخلفائِه وأصحابِه وأئمةِ أهلِ بيتهِ - مثل الإمامِ علي بن الحسين زين العابدين، وابنِه الإمام أبي جعفر محمد بن علي الباقر، وابنِه الإمام أبي عبد الله جعفر بن محمد الصادق شيخ علماء الأمة - ومثل مالك بن أنس والثوري وطبقتهما، وجدَ ذلك جميعَه متفقًا مجتمعًا في أصولِ دينهم وجماع شريعتهم.

ووجدَ في ذلك ما يَشْغَلُه وما يُغْنِيْه عما أحدثَه كثيرٌ من المَتأخرين من أنواع المقالات التي تخالف ما كان عليه أولئك السلف ممن ينتصب لعداوَةِ آلِ بيتِ رسولِ الله ﷺ، ويَبْخَسُهم حقوقَهم ويُؤذيهم، أو ممن يَغلُو فيهم غير الحق، ويَفترِي عليهم الكذبَ، ويَبخَسُ السابقين والطائعين حقوقَهم.

---

against the righteous predecessors and companions of the Prophet. One of the main reasons why these schools profess love of *Ahlulbayt* yet oppose each other in a variety of theological and juridical matters is because their sources are replete with contradictory forgeries and fabrications in the name of *Ahlulbayt*. This preponderance of lies and fallacies that manifests differently in each of these Shi'ite sects is a highlight of them, as was mentioned by Ibn Taymiyya.

One who adheres to these traditions from the aforementioned forebears, concerning *Tawḥīd*, Allah's attributes, divine justice (*al-ʿAdl*) and *Qadar*, *Īmān*, theological categorizations of people (*al-Asmāʾ wa-l-Aḥkām*), threat of punishment for sin (*al-waʿīd*), reward for good deeds (*al-thawāb*), punishment for sin (*al-ʿadhāb*), enjoinment of good (*al-amr bi-l-maʿrūf*), forbidding of evil (*al-nahī ʿan al-munkar*), and other related rulings such as those pertaining to righteous and wicked rulers, their subjects, and the *Ṣaḥāba* and kin [of the Prophet], will discern that there is sufficient evidence for any rational individual to recognize there was no discord among the aforementioned predecessors on these matters. Their only forms of disagreement were those sanctioned by the Quran and the *Sunnah*, as was previously discussed.(1)

In a similar vein, the follower of these traditions will note that the grave innovations (*bidaʿ*), which conflict with the Quran, the *Sunnah*, and the consensus of the guided and guiding scholars, were only introduced by later figures. These figures may attribute some of these innovations to certain predecessors, either through unreliable transmission or by interpretation of some of the predecessors' ambiguous statements.

Moreover, it is by the mercy of Allah that whenever such beliefs are attributed to the predecessors, it is rare to not find decisive and explicit traditions from them through reliable and established transmission which demonstrate the error of those who had erred in transmission or interpretation. That is because the straight path with respect to the entire *Ummah* is analogous to the straight path with respect to the other religions.

---

(1) I am in the process of compiling a large book that embodies the authentic traditions from *Ahlulbayt* on a host of key theological matters, and I can comfortably state that Ibn Taymiyya's characterization of reality is quite accurate. The early nobles and scholars of *Ahlulbayt* were upon mainstream Islam, and their doctrines and creeds were indistinguishable from those of other mainstream Islamic scholarship at the time.

ورأى أنَ في المأثور عن أولئك السلف في باب التوحيد والصفات، وباب العدل والقدر، وباب الإيمان والأسماء والأحكام، وباب الوعيد والثَّواب والعذاب، وبابَ الأمر بالمعروف والنهي عن المنكَر، وما يتصل به من حكم الأمراَء أبرارِهم وفُجَّارِهم، وحكم الرعيَّةِ معهم، والكلام في الصحابة والقرابة ما يُبيِّنُ لكل عاقلٍ عادلٍ أنَّ السلفَ المذكورين لم يكن بينهم من النزاع في هذه الأبواب إلا من جنسِ النزاع الذي أقرَّهم عليه الكتاب والسنةَ كما تقدَّم ذكرُه.

وأنَّ البدعَ الغليظةَ المخالفةَ للكتابِ والسنةِ واتفاقِ أولي الأمر الهداةِ المهتدين إنّما حَدَثَتْ من الأخلاف، وقد يَعزُونَ بعضَ ذلك إلى بعض الأسلاف، تارةً بنقل غيرِ ثابتٍ، وتارةً بتأويلٍ لشيءٍ من كلامهم متشابهٍ.

ثمَّ إن من رحمة الله أنه قَلَّ أن يُنقَل عنهم شيء من ذلك إلا وفي النقول الصحيحة الثابتة عنهم للقولِ المحكم الصريحِ ما يُبيِّنُ غلط الغالطين عليهم في النقل أو التأويل، وهذا لأن الصراط المستقيم في كل الأمة بمنزلة الصراط في المِلَل.

The perfection of Islam lies in the middle ground between religions and faiths, just as Allah has stated, "And thus We have made you a moderate community [Quran 2: 143]," meaning that they did not deviate towards the extremes, like the Jews, Christians and the Mandaeans.

Similarly, the people of uprightness and adherence to the Messenger of Allah's ﷺ *Sunnah* and the path of the *Salaf* grasped onto moderation and did not swerve towards the extremes. As an example, the Jews harbored animosity towards the prophets and the sincere to the extent that they murdered and impugned them. As Allah said, "You impugned some and murdered others. [Quran 2:87]" On the other hand, the Christians countered them by granting the priests and monks authority to mandate and prohibit within religion as they deemed fit. In a similar vein, they (the Jews and Christians) counter each other in the remainder of matters.

Allah thus guided the believers to moderation. They held the prophets in the esteem they truly deserved, and they revered them, aided them, loved them, obeyed them, and followed them. They neither rejected the prophets like the Jews nor did they excessively praise them and exceed the proper limits in their veneration by attributing divinity to them like the Christians.

Akin to this is the issue of abrogation. The believers held the belief that it was within Allah's prerogative to abrogate, and they forbade anyone else from doing so. The creation is Allah's and the command is his. Just as none other than Allah can create, only He can mandate.

فكمالُ الإسلام هو الوسَطُ في الأديان والمِلَل، كما قال تعالى: (وَكَذَلِكَ جَعَلْنَاكُمْ أُمَّةً وَسَطاً)، لم ينحرفوا انحرافَ اليهود والنصارى والصابئين.

فكذلك أهلُ الاستقامةِ ولزومِ سنة رسولِ الله ﷺ وما عليه السلف، تمسَّكوا بالوسط ولم ينحرفوا إلى الأطراف. فاليهود مثلاً جَفَوا في الأنبياء والصديقين حتى قتلوهم وكذَّبوهم، كما قال الله تعالى: (فَفَرِيقاً كَذَّبْتُمْ وَفَرِيقاً تَقْتُلُونَ). والنصارى غَلَوا فيهم حتى عَبَدوهم، كما قال تعالى: (يَا أَهْلَ الْكِتَابِ لا تَغْلُوا فِي دِينِكُمْ وَلا تَقُولُوا عَلَى اللَّهِ إِلَّا الْحَقَّ) الآية. والنصارى قابَلُوهم فجوَّزوا للقِسّيسين والرهبان أن يُوجِبوا ما شاءوا ويُحرِّموا ما شاءوا. وكذلك تَقَابُلهم في سائر الأمور.

فهدى الله المؤمنين إلى الوسط، فاعتقدوا في الأنبياء ما يستحقونه ووقَّروهم وعَزَّروهم وأحبُّوهم وأطاعوهم واتبعوهم، ولم يردُّوهم كما فعلت اليهود. ولا أَطْرَوهم ولا غَلَوا فيهم فنزَّلوهم منزلةَ الربوبية كما فعلت النصارى.

وكذلك في النَّسْخ، جوَّزوا أن ينسخ الله ولم يُجوِّزوا لغيره أن ينسخ، فإنّ الله له الخلق والأمر. فكما لا يَخلُق غيرُه لا يأمُر غيرُه.

Similarly, the people of uprightness in Islam who hold fast to the Prophetic wisdom and infallibility of consensus are the middle ground in matters of *Tawḥīd* and Allah's attributes between the negating deniers of Allah's attributes and the anthropomorphists. Furthermore, with regards to matters of *Qadar*, divine justice (*al-ʿAdl*), and the actions of the creation, they are the middle ground between the Indeterminist Qadariyya (*al-Qadariyya al-Majūsiyya*) and the Determinist Qadariyya (*al-Qadariyya al-Jabriyya).*

And in matters pertaining to the categorization and classification of individuals, they are the middle ground between those who exclude sinners entirely from the faith, as did the Kharijites and the Muʿtazilites, and those who equate the faith of an impious person (*fāsiq*) with that of the prophets and the righteous, as did the Murjiʾa and the Jahmites. Furthermore, with regards to Allah's warning of punishment for sins (*al-waʿīd*), reward, and retribution, they are the middle ground between the *Waʿīdīyyīn*, who do not profess our prophet's intercession (*shafāʿa*) for major sinners, and the Murjiʾa who deny the implementation of punishment for disobedience.

In matters pertaining to governance, enjoining the good, and forbidding the evil, they are the middle ground, avoiding the extremes of those who condone the transgressions and sins of the rulers and incline towards the oppressors, and those who refuse to cooperate with anyone in any virtuous conduct and moral principles, avoiding *jihād*, Friday prayer, and Eids if the ruler is not infallible, only adhering to Allah and His messenger's commands when obeying a nonexistent being.(1)

---

(1) Ibn Taymiyya is referring to Shi'ites who refuse to partake in virtuous administrative duties of governance with Muslim rulers, such as *jihād*, congregational prayers, and religious festivities, in the absence of a "rightful *Imām*."

This is reminiscent of the story of an ex-Zaydi Shi'ite scholar from the past century, Aḥmed ibn ʿAbdillāh al-Jandārī (d. 1337/1919) who used to avoid congregational Friday prayers in Ṣanʿāʾ, Yemen, during Ottoman rule. One day, while walking near a mosque after Friday prayer, a man approached him

وهكذا أهلُ الاستقامةِ في الإسلام المعتصمون بالحكمةِ النبوية والعصمة الجماعية متوسطون في باب التوحيد والصفات بين النفاة المعطِّلة وبين المشبِّهة الممثِّلة، وفي باب القدر والعدل والأفعال بين القدرية الجبرية والقدرية المجوسية.

وفي باب الأسماء والأحكام بين من أخرجَ أهل المعاصي من الإيمان بالكلية كالخوارج وأهل المنزلة، وبين من جَعَلَ إيمان الفُسَّاق كإيمان الأنبياء والصديقين كالمرجئة والجهمية. وفي باب الوعيد والثواب والعقاب بين الوعيديِّين الذين لا يقولون بشفاعة نبينا لأهل الكبائر، وبين المرجئة الذين لا يقولون بنفود الوعيد.

وفي باب الإمامة والأمر بالمعروف والنهي عن المنكر بين الذين يُوافِقون الولاةَ على الإثم والعدوان ويَركَنون إلى الذين ظلموا، وبين الذين لا يرون أن يُعاوِنوا أحدًا على البرّ والتقوى لا على جهادٍ ولا جمعةٍ ولا أعيادٍ إلا أن يكون معصومًا ولا يَدخُلوا فيما أمر الله به ورسولُه إلا في طاعةِ من لا وجودَ له.

---

and sarcastically remarked, "These congregants are supposed to enter the Hellfire for praying the Friday prayer, yet you alone are supposed to enter Heaven for not praying with them and believing that it is only obligatory within the jurisdiction of an *Imām*?!"

These words touched al-Jandārī, leading to his revision of his beliefs, which eventually culminated in him seeing a dream. Al-Jandārī reported that he saw a dream in Jumādā al-Ākhira of the year 1320 A.H. where he was praying with a congregation in the Grand Mosque of Kūfa behind ʿAlī ibn Abī Ṭālib, yet he was unable to see his face. He thus was further inclined to abandon his *bidʿa,* and he eventually repented. See Mawsūʿat Aʿlām al-Qarn al-Rābiʿ ʿAshar wal-Khāmis ʿAshar (p. 487-489).

The former group, in their obedience to the rulers, engage in prohibited things, while the latter group abandons religious obligations and rulings. The extremists from the latter group abandon the religious ordinances to oppose whoever they deem an oppressor, though that person may actually be thorough in his knowledge and justice.

The people of rectitude and justice obey Allah and His Messenger to the best of their capacity. They act righteously to the best of their ability, and they follow the commands of the Messenger to the best of their ability. They do not forsake their religious obligations as a reaction to someone else engaging in prohibited acts. Rather, they are as Allah described, "O you who have believed! You are responsible for your own souls. He who has gone astray cannot harm you if you are guided. [Quran 5:105]"

They do not collaborate with anyone to sin, and they do not remove evil by replacing it with a worse evil. They only enjoin the good through good means. They are moderate in all matters, and that is why the Prophet ﷺ described them as the "saved group" when speaking of his nation's fragmentation and discord.(1)

[The Significance of the Day of ʿĀshurāʾ]

Among these matters is the day of ʿĀshūrāʾ in which Allah honored His Prophet's grandson, one of the two masters of the youth of paradise, with martyrdom at the hands of wicked and wretched murderers. It was a grave calamity among the greatest calamities to have befallen Islam.

---

(1) Musnad Aḥmed ibn Ḥanbal (14/124, 19/241, 19/462)

فالأوَّلون يدخلون في المحرَّمات، وهؤلاء يتركون واجباتِ الدين وشرائعَ الإسلام، وغُلاتُهم يتركونَها لأجل موافقةِ من يظنونه ظالمًا، وقد يكون كاملاً في علمه وعدلِه.

وأهلُ الاستقامة والاعتدال يُطيعون الله ورسوله بحسب الإمكان، فيتقون اللهَ ما استطاعوا، وإذا أمرهم الرسولُ بأمرٍ أتوا منه ما استطاعوا. ولا يتركون ما أُمِروا به لفعلِ غيرِهم ما نُهِيَ عنه، بل كما قال تعالى: ﴿يَا أَيُّهَا الَّذِينَ آمَنُوا عَلَيْكُمْ أَنْفُسَكُمْ لا يَضُرُّكُمْ مَنْ ضَلَّ إِذَا اهْتَدَيْتُمْ﴾.

ولا يُعاوِنون أحدًا على معصية، ولا يُزيلون المنكرَ بما هو أنكرُ منه، ولا يأمرون بالمعروف إلا بالمعروف. فهم وَسَط في عامة الأمور، ولهذا وصفهم النبي ﷺ بأنهم الطائفة الناجية لما ذكر اختلاف أمته وافتراقهم.

ومن ذلك أن اليوم الذي هو يومُ عاشوراء الذي أكرمَ الله فيه سِبطَ نبيِّه وأحدَ سيِّدَي شباب أهل الجنة بالشهادة على أيدي مَن قَتلَه من الفَجَرة الأشقياء، وكان ذلك مصيبة عظيمة من أعظم المصائب الواقعة في الإسلام.

Imām Aḥmed and others reported from Fāṭima bint al-Ḥusayn, a witness of her father's murder, from her father al-Ḥusayn ibn ʿAlī (may Allah be pleased with them), from his grandfather the Messenger of Allah ﷺ that he said, "When a person who has been struck by a calamity remembers it, even if it is old, and then says, 'verily, we belong to Allah and to Him we shall return,' Allah will reward him with the same reward that was given to him on the day of his calamity."(1)

Allah was aware that such calamities would be remembered with the progression of time, so it was from the charms of Islam that this ḥadīth was first transmitted by the very person struck by the calamity.

Undoubtedly, Allah's treatment of al-Ḥusayn was an honor to him (may Allah be pleased with him), an elevation of his status before Allah, a delivery of his rank to the ranks of the martyrs, and a means for him to join members of his household who were subjected to a variety of tribulations.

Al-Ḥasan and al-Ḥusayn had not experienced the same degree of tribulations that their grandfather, mother and uncle had endured. That is because they were both born during the zenith of Islam and raised within the embrace of the believers. However, Allah perfected his blessings upon them through martyrdom, with one falling victim to poisoning and the other being murdered. That is because Allah has high ranks within His abode of honor that only the people of tribulation (*ibtilāʾ*) are able to attain.

---

(1) Musnad Aḥmed ibn Ḥanbal (3/256-257)

وقد روى الإمام أحمد وغيره عن فاطمة بنت الحسين - وقد كانت قد شهدتْ مصرعَ أبيها - عن أبيها الحسين بن علي رضي الله عنهم، عن جدِّه رسولِ الله ﷺ أنه قال: "ما من رجل يُصابُ بمصيبةٍ فيذكُر مصيبتَه وإن قدمتْ، فيُحدِثُ لها استرجاعًا، إلا أعطاه الله من الأجر مثل أجره يومَ أُصِيبَ بها."

فقد علم الله أنّ مثل هذه المصيبة العظيمة سيتجدد ذكرُها مع تقادُمِ العهد، فكان من محاسن الإسلام أن روى هذا الحديثَ صاحبُ المصيبةِ والمُصَابُ به أوّلاً.

ولا ريبَ أن ذلك إنما فعلَه الله كرامةً للحسين رضي الله عنه، ورفعًا لدرجتِه ومنزلتِه عند الله، وتبليغًا له مَنازلَ الشهداء، وإلحاقًا له بأهل بيته الذين ابتُلُوا بأصنافِ البلاء.

ولم يكن الحسن والحسين حصلَ لهما من الابتلاءِ ما حَصَلَ لجدِّهما ولأمّهما وعَمِّهما، لأنهما وُلِدا في عِزِّ الإسلام وتَربَّيا في حُجور المؤمنين، فأتمَّ الله نعمتَه عليهما بالشهادة، أحدهما مسمومًا والآخر مقتولاً. لأنّ الله عنده من المنازل العالية في دار كرامته ما لا ينالها إلا أهلُ البلاء.

As the Messenger of Allah ﷺ was once asked, "Who are the most tribulated people?" He replied, "The prophets, then the righteous, then those nearest to them. A person is tribulated in proportion to his faith: The stronger the faith, the greater the trials, and the weaker the faith, the lesser the trials. A believer is tested frequently until he eventually reaches a state where he treads on the earth without a single sin."(1) Those who either aided in al-Ḥusayn's murder or approved of it were consequently wretched.

[Some Islamic Guidelines on Grief Vis-à-Vis ʿĀshūrā']

What Allah prescribed for the believers when they are struck with calamities, even if severe, is that they say, "To Allah we belong, and to Him we will return (*innā li-llāh wa-innā ilayhī rājiʿūn*). [Quran 2:156]"

In his *Musnad*, al-Shāfiʿī reported that upon the Prophet's demise, when his family was struck with that calamity, they heard a voice calling out, "O household of the Messenger of Allah! In Allah is solace from every calamity, recompense from every lost person, and a retrieval of all that is lost! So have trust and hope in Allah! For indeed, the truly afflicted one is the one who is deprived of earning reward!" They were of the belief that it was al-Khaḍir who had come to offer his condolences for the Prophet's demise.(2)

---

(1) Musnad Aḥmed ibn Ḥanbal (3/78, 3/87, 3/128, 3/159)

(2) Musnad al-Shāfiʿī (p. 361). This tradition is authentically attributed to Jaʿfar al-Ṣādiq, who reported it from his father, al-Bāqir. See Kitāb al-Ṭabaqāt al-Kabīr of Ibn Saʿd (2/239), al-Mustadrak of al-Ḥākim (3/59), and al-Maṭālib al-ʿĀliya (17/526).

The discontinuity between al-Bāqir and the original eyewitness of this account would render it weak in the eyes of the ḥadīth critics, and Ibn Taymiyya is acutely aware of that. I believe he cites the report here for several plausible reasons: (1) its essence and core teachings are sound and present in other reliable texts, and (2) it involves the Prophet's household, making it particularly relevant to a Shi'ite audience. Perhaps he was also inclined to cite it here since it was reported by Jaʿfar al-Ṣādiq and his father, though he does not make note of this whilst citing the tradition.

كما قال النبي ﷺ وقد سُئِلَ: أيُّ الناسِ أشدُّ بلاءً؟ فقال: "الأنبياء ثمّ الصالحون ثمّ الأمثل فالأمثل، يُبتَلى الرجلُ على حسبِ دينه، فإن كان في دينه صَلابة زِيْدَ في بلائه، وإن كان في دينه رِقّةٌ خُفِّف عنه. ولا يزال البلاءُ بالمؤمنِ حتى يَمشي على الأرضِ وليس عليه خطيئةٌ." وشَقِيَ بقتلِه من أعانَ عليه أو رضي به.

فالذي شرعَه الله للمؤمنين عند الإصابة بالمصائب وإن عظُمتْ أن يقولوا: إنّا لله وإنا إليه راجعون.

وقد روى الشافعي في مسنده أن النبي ﷺ لما ماتَ وأصاب أهلَ بيته من المصيبة ما أصابَهم، سمعوا قائلاً يقول: "يا آلَ بيتِ رسول الله! إنّ في الله عَزَاءً من كلّ مصيبةٍ، وخَلَفًا من كل هالك، ودَرَكًا من كل فائت، فبالله فثِقُوا وإيَّاه فارْجُوا، فإن المُصَابَ من حُرِمَ الثوابَ." فكانوا يرونه الخضر جاء يُعزِّيهم بالنبي ﷺ.

As for partaking in mourning ceremonies during times of calamities and then commemorating their anniversaries as mourning ceremonies, that is not rooted in the religion of Islam. It is a matter not practiced by the Messenger of Allah ﷺ, nor by any of the righteous forerunners, nor by any of their later followers in righteousness, and it is not from the traditions of *Ahlulbayt* and others.

ʿAlī's family witnessed his murder, and al-Ḥusayn's murder was witnessed by some from his family. Many years passed since then, yet they remained steadfastly adherent to the *Sunnah* of the Messenger of Allah ﷺ, refusing to initiate mourning ceremonies or wailings. Instead, they remained patient and said, "To Allah we belong, and to Him we will return," as was mandated by Allah and His Messenger.

Or, they may grieve permissibly with crying and heartache in the immediate aftermath of the calamity. As the Messenger of Allah ﷺ said, "Whatever emanates from the heart and eyes is from Allah, and whatever is carried out by the hand or uttered by the tongue is from the Shayṭān."(1) And he ﷺ said, "He who strikes his cheeks, tears his clothes, and makes the calls of the *Jāhiliyya* is not one of us."(2) What he meant by the calls of the *Jāhiliyya* is like when the afflicted person shouts out [about the deceased], "My supporter! My helper! My rock!"

And he ﷺ said, "The wailing woman who does not repent prior to her death will be clothed with a shirt made of tar and a garment made of mange on the Day of Resurrection."(3) He ﷺ also said, "May Allah curse the wailing woman and the woman who listens to her."(4)

---

(1) Musnad Aḥmed ibn Ḥanbal (4/30-31)
(2) Ṣaḥīḥ al-Bukhārī (2/81), Ṣaḥīḥ Muslim (1/99)
(3) Ṣaḥīḥ Muslim (2/644)
(4) Musnad Aḥmed ibn Ḥanbal (18/166)

فأما اتخاذ المآتم في المصائب واتخاذ أوقاتها مآتمَ فليس من دين الإسلام، وهو أمر لم يفعله رسول الله ﷺ ولا أحد من السابقين الأولين ولا من التابعين لهم بإحسان، ولا من عادة أهل البيت ولا غيرهم.

وقد شَهِدَ مقتلَ عليٍّ أهلُ بيته، وشهدَ مقتلَ الحسين من شهدَه من أهل بيته، وقد مرَّتْ على ذلك سنون كثيرة وهم متمسكون بسنة رسول الله ﷺ، لا يُحدِثون مأتمًا ولا نياحةً، بل يصبرون ويسترجعون كما أمر الله ورسولُه.

أو يفعلون ما لا بأسَ به من الحزن والبكاء عند قرب المصيبة. قال النبي ﷺ: "ما كان من العين والقلب فمن الله، وما كان من اليد واللسان فمن الشيطان." وقال: "ليس منا من لَطَم الخدودَ وشَقَّ الجيوبَ ودَعا بدعوى الجاهلية"، يعني مثل قول المُصاب: يا سَنَداه! يا ناصراه! يا عَضُداه!

وقال ﷺ: "إن النائحةَ إذا لم تَتُبْ قبلَ موتها فإنها تُلْبَسُ يومَ القيامة دِرعًا من جَرَبٍ وسِرْبالاً مَن قَطِرانٍ." وقال: "لعن الله النائحةَ والمستمعةَ إليها."

Allah said in His revelation, "O prophet! If believing women come to you, pledging allegiance to you, on condition that they will not associate anything with God, nor steal, nor commit adultery, nor murder their children, nor commit perjury as to parenthood, nor disobey you in anything righteous, then accept their allegiance and pray to Allah for their forgiveness. Allah is Forgiving and Merciful. [Quran 60:12]"

The Messenger of Allah ﷺ explained that Allah's statement, "nor disobey you in anything righteous," is a reference to wailing.(1) The Messenger of Allah ﷺ also disassociated from the *ḥāliqa* and the *ṣāliqa*.(2) The *ḥāliqa* is the woman who shaves her hair off at times of adversity, while the *ṣāliqa* is the woman who raises her voice at times of adversity.

Jarīr ibn ʿAbdillāh said, "We used to associate congregating at the grieving family's house and them preparing food for the visitors with wailing."(3) Rather, it is the *Sunnah* to prepare food for the grieving family, for they are preoccupied by their calamity. As the Messenger of Allah said when Jaʿfar ibn Abī Ṭālib's martyrdom at the Battle of Mu'ta was announced, "Prepare food for Jaʿfar's family, for they are facing something that preoccupies them."(4)

Similar to that is what some other people do on ʿAshūrāʾ, such as the application of kohl to the eyes, the dyeing of hair, handshakes, or the performance of *ghusl*. This too is an innovation (*bidʿa*) that has no basis, and it was not mentioned by any of the aforementioned *Imāms*. Rather, there is a ḥadīth that was reported about it which says, "Whoever performs *ghusl* on the Day of ʿĀshūrāʾ shall not fall ill in that year, and whoever applies kohl to his eyes shall not have sore eyes in that year," and similar things.(5)

---

(1) Ṣaḥīḥ Muslim (2/646)
(2) Ṣaḥīḥ al-Bukhārī (2/81), Ṣaḥīḥ Muslim (1/100)
(3) Musnad Aḥmed ibn Ḥanbal (11/505)
(4) Musnad Aḥmed ibn Ḥanbal (3/280), al-Mustadrak ʿalā al-Ṣaḥīḥayn (1/527)
(5) Ibn al-Jawzī said, "Any person with reason would not doubt that this ḥadīth is fabricated..." See Kitāb al-Mawḍūʿāt of Ibn al-Jawzī (2/200-201).

وقد قال في تنزيله: (يَا أَيُّهَا النَّبِيُّ إِذَا جَاءَكَ الْمُؤْمِنَاتُ يُبَايِعْنَكَ عَلَى أَنْ لا يُشْرِكْنَ بِاللَّهِ شَيْئاً وَلا يَسْرِقْنَ وَلا يَزْنِينَ وَلا يَقْتُلْنَ أَوْلادَهُنَّ وَلا يَأْتِينَ بِبُهْتَانٍ يَفْتَرِينَهُ بَيْنَ أَيْدِيهِنَّ وَأَرْجُلِهِنَّ وَلا يَعْصِينَكَ فِي مَعْرُوفٍ فَبَايِعْهُنَّ وَاسْتَغْفِرْ لَهُنَّ اللَّهَ إِنَّ اللَّهَ غَفُورٌ رَحِيمٌ).

وقد فسَّر النبي ﷺ قوله (وَلا يَعْصِينَكَ فِي مَعْرُوفٍ) بأنها النياحة. وتبرَّأ النبيّ ﷺ من الحالقة والصالقة. والحالقة: التي تَحلِق شعرَها عند المصيبة، والصالقة: التي ترفع صوتَها عند المصيبة.

وقال جرير بن عبد الله: "كنا نعدُّ الاجتماعَ إلى أهل الميت وصَنْعَتهم الطعامَ للناس من النياحة." وإنما السنةُ أن يُصنَع لأهل الميت طعامٌ، لأنّ مصيبتَهم تَشْغَلُهم، كما قال النبي ﷺ لما نُعِيَ جعفر بن أبي طالب لما استشهد بمؤتةَ فقال: "اصنَعوا لآلِ جعفرٍ طعامًا، فقد جاءهم ما يَشْغَلُهم."

وهكذا ما يفعل قوم آخرون يوم عاشوراءَ من الاكتحال والاختضاب أو المصافحة والاغتسال، فهو بدعة أيضًا لا أصلَ لها، ولم يذكرها أحد من الأئمة المشهورين، وإنما رُوِي فيها حديث "من اغتسلَ يومَ عاشوراءَ لم يَمرض تلك السنةَ، ومن اكتحلَ يومَ عاشوراء لم يَرمَدْ ذلك العام" ونحو ذلك.

Some of those who heard this ḥadīth believed it was authentic, and they thus acted upon it. However, this ḥadīth is considered weak and baseless according to the people of knowledge. None of this practice was transmitted from the Prophet, the righteous forerunners, or their successors (*al-tābiʿīn*).

However, what is established from the Prophet ﷺ is that he observed fasting on ʿĀshūrāʾ and encouraged others to do the same, stating that such an act absolves one year's worth of sins. The Messenger of Allah expounded that on this very day, Allah had saved Moses and his people and drowned Pharaoh and his people.(1) It has also been reported that the significant events of all nations occurred within this day. Thus, it is among Allah's honors to al-Ḥusayn that he ordained his martyrdom to occur on this day.

Allah may simultaneously bestow a blessing that necessitates gratitude and present a trial that calls for patience. This is exemplified in how the seventeenth of Ramaḍān was the day in which the Battle of Badr took place while also being the day ʿAlī was murdered. Of even greater significance is how Monday in the month of Rabīʿ al-Awwal is the day of the Messenger of Allah's birth and migration (*hijra*), yet it also is the day on which he died.

The believing slave is afflicted with pleasing circumstances and disheartening trials simultaneously so that he may be thankful and patient. How then should he be if he were to face one of those circumstances on two separate occasions?

It is recommended that one observes fasting on the ninth and tenth days [of Muḥarram], and it not recommended that he applies kohl [to his eyes]. The believers who do apply kohl to their eyes on ʿĀshūrāʾ are not acting out of hostility to *Ahlulbayt*, though they are erroneous in their actions. However, if any of them intends to taunt *Ahlulbayt* through such practices or finds joy in their plights, then let the curse of Allah, the angels and all of humanity be upon them.

---

(1) Ṣaḥīḥ al-Bukhārī (3/44), Ṣaḥīḥ Muslim (2/795, 2/818-819)

فاعتقد بعض من سمعه أنه حديث صحيح فعملوا به. وهذا حديث ضعيف عند أهل العلم لا أصل له، ولم ينقل عن النبي ﷺ ولا عن السابقين والتابعين شيء من ذلك.

ولكن الذي ثبت عن النبي ﷺ أنه صامَ يومَ عاشوراءَ وأمرَ بصيامه، وقال: "صومُه يُكفر سنةً." وقرّر النبي ﷺ أن الله أنجىَ فيه موسى وقومَه وأغرقَ فرعونَ وقومَه. ورُوِيَ أنه كان فيه حوادث الأمم، فمن كرامة الحسين أن الله جعلَ استشهادَه فيه.

وقد يجمع الله في الوقت شخصًا أو نوعًا من النعمة التي تُوجب شكرًا أو المحنة التي تُوجِب صبرًا، كما أنّ سابعَ عشر شَهر رمضان فيه كانت وقعةُ بدرٍ، وفيه كان مقتلُ عليّ. وأبلغ من ذلك أن يوم الاثنين في ربيع الأول مولد النبي ﷺ، وفيه هجرته، وفيه وفاته.

والعبد المؤمن يُبتَلى بالحسناتِ التي تَسُرُّهُ والسيئاتِ التي تَسُوءُه في الوقت الواحد ليكون صبَّارًا شكورًا، فكيف إذا وقعَ مثلُ ذلك في وقتين متعددين من نوع واحد؟

ويُستحب صومُ التاسع والعاشر، ولا يُستحبُّ الكحلُ. والذين يصنعونَ من الكحل من أهل الدين لا يقصدون به مناصبة أهل البيت – وإن كانوا مخطئين في فعلهم. ومَن قَصدَ منهم أهلَ البيت بذلك أو غيره، أو فرحَ أو استشفَى بمصائبهم، فعليه لعنة الله والملائكة والناس أجمعين.

For the Messenger of Allah ﷺ, upon hearing al-ʿAbbās' complaint that some from Quraysh has ostracized Banī Hāshim, said, "By the One in Whose grasp lies my soul, they shall not enter Paradise until they love you in my honor."(1) The Messenger of Allah ﷺ also said, "Allah has chosen Quraysh from among Banī Kināna; and he chose Banī Hāshim from among Quraysh; and he chose me from Banī Hāshim."(2) It has also been reported that he ﷺ said, "Love Allah for His bounties with which He nourishes you. Love me out of your love of Allah, and love my family as an extension of your love for me."(3) This is a vast subject where much more can be said.

[What Prompted Ibn Taymiyya to Write this Letter]

The reason behind this letter is that a brother approached me with a document which contained references to the Messenger of Allah ﷺ and the nobles of *Ahlulbayt* as well as oaths related to the shrine of the awaited Mahdī. In response, this individual was informed about the merits and rights of *Ahlulbayt* in a manner that warmed his heart and made him comfortable. The earlier portions of this letter touched upon some of the obligations towards them, and though there is much more to be said on this topic, this carrier [of the letter] could not bear further exposition.

This individual was also engaged in discussion about certain aspects of genealogies and oaths that must be known within Allah's religion. As a result, he requested a letter to be composed for his companions, with whom he intends to reunite. For the Messenger of Allah ﷺ has said, "Faith is sincerity (*al-naṣīḥa*)." The Prophet ﷺ was then asked, "Towards whom, O Messenger of Allah?" He replied, "Towards Allah, His Book, His Messenger, and to the rulers of the Muslims and their laity."(4)

---

(1) Al-Jāmiʿ al-Kabīr of al-Tirmidhī (6/110), Muṣannaf Ibn Abī Shayba (17/182)
(2) Ṣaḥīḥ Muslim (4/1782)
(3) Al-Jāmiʿ al-Kabīr of al-Tirmidhī (6/134)
(4) Ṣaḥīḥ Muslim (1/74)

فقد قال النبي ﷺ: "والذي نفسي بيده لا يدخلون الجنةَ حتى يُحبّوكم من أجلي"، لما شَكَا إليه العباس أن بعض قريش يَجْفُون بني هاشم. وقال ﷺ: "إن الله اصطفى قريشًا من بني كنانة، واصطفى بني هاشم من قريش، واصطفاني من بني هاشمِ." ورُوِيَ عنه أنه ﷺ قال: "أَحِبُّوا الله لما يَغذُوكم به من نِعَمِه، وأحبُّوني لحبّ الله، وأَحِبُّوا أهلَ بيتي لحبّي." وهذا باب واسع يطولُ القول فيه.

وكان سببُ هذه المواصلة أن بعض الإخوان قَدِمَ بورقةٍ فيها ذِكرُ النبي ﷺ وذِكر سادة أهلِ البيت، وقد أُجري فيها ذِكرُ النذور لمشهد المنتظر. فخُوطِبَ مِن فضائل أهل البيت وحقوقِهم بما سَرَّ قلبَه وشَرحَ صَدْرَه، وكان ما ذُكِر بعضَ الواجب، فإن الكلام في هذا طويل، ولم يحتمل هذا الحامل أكثر من ذلك.

وخُوطِبَ فيما يتعلق بالأنساب والنذور بما يجب في دين الله، فسأَلَ المكاتبةَ بذلك إلى من يذهب إليه من الإخوان، فإنّ النبي ﷺ قال: "الدين النصيحة." قالوا: "لمن يا رسولَ الله؟" قال: "لله ولكتابه ولرسوله ولأئمة المسلمين وعامتهم."

[Historical and Genealogical Errors in the Document]

Regarding the document on genealogies and dates, it has errors in several instances, such as the claim that the Prophet ﷺ died in the month of Rajab; and that he is Muḥammad son of ʿAbdullāh son ʿAbdilMuṭṭalib son of ʿAmr son of al-ʿAlāʾ son of Hāshim; and that Jaʿfar al-Ṣādiq died during the reign of Hārūn al-Rashīd, among other errors.

There is a consensus among the scholars that the Prophet ﷺ died in the month of Rabīʿ al-Awwal, the month in which he was born and deceased. It also agreed upon that he was born and deceased on Monday and that prophethood was revealed to him on Monday as well. Furthermore, it is also agreed upon that his grandfather is Hāshim son of ʿAbdManāf and that Hāshim was named ʿAmr and referred to as ʿAmr al-ʿUlā, as was stated by the poet, "عمرو العلا هَشَمَ الثريد لقومه ورجال مكة مُسْنِتون عجاف." It is also agreed upon that Jaʿfar Abū ʿAbdillāh [al-Ṣādiq] died in the year 148 during the reign of Abū Jaʿfar al-Manṣūr.

[On the Alleged Mahdī of the Twelver Shia]

Regarding the awaited Mahdī, a group of scholars specializing in the genealogies of *Ahlulbayt* have noted that al-Ḥasan al-ʿAskarī did not leave behind any descendants upon his passing.(1)

---

(1) This conclusion is not exclusive to mainstream Islam. Rather, it was also upheld by scholars from other schools as well. Many non-Twelver Shi'ite sects at the time rejected al-Ḥasan al-ʿAskarī's imamate and/or the notion that he had fathered a son prior to his death. Refer to my book, Schisms of the Shia: A Series of Illustrations (p. 9, 11).

Among the renowned scholars of mainstream Islam, al-Ṭabarī (d. 310), Yaḥyā ibn Ṣāʿid (d. 318), Ibn Qāniʿ (d. 351) and Ibn Ḥazm (d. 456) and others noted that al-Ḥasan al-ʿAskarī died without fathering any children. See Siyar Aʿlām al-Nubalāʾ (13/121-122) and Minhāj al-Sunnah al-Nabawiyya of Ibn Taymiyya (1/122).

Among the Zaydi Shia, the renowned Zaydi Imām, al-Nāṣir al-Uṭrūsh (d. 304), maintained that al-Ḥasan al-ʿAskarī died without fathering any children.

أما ورقة الأنساب والتواريخ ففيها غلطٌ في مواضع متعددة، مثل ذكرِه أن النبي ﷺ توفي في صفر، وأنه محمد بن عبد الله بن عبد المطلب ابن عمرو بن العلاء بن هاشم، وأنّ جعفر الصادق توفي في خلافة الرشيد، وغير ذلك.

فإنه لا خلاف بين أهل العلم أن النبي ﷺ توفي في شهرِ ربيع الأول شهرِ مولده وشهرِ هجرته، وأنه توفي يوم الاثنين، وفيه وُلِد وفيه أُنزِل عليه. وجدُّه هاشم بن عبد مناف، وإنما كان هاشم يُسمَّى عمرًا، ويقال له عمرو العلا، كما قال الشاعر:

عَمرو العُلا هَشَمَ الثَّرِيدَ لقومِه ورجالُ مكَّةَ مُسنِتُون عِجَافُ

وأن جعفرًا أبا عبد الله توفي في سنة ثمانٍ وأربعين في إمارة أبي جعفر المنصور.

وأما المنتظَر فقد ذكر طائفة من أهل العلم بأنسابِ أهلِ البيت أن الحسن بن علي العسكري لما توفي بعسكر سامَرَّاء لم يُعقِب ولم ينسل.

Al-Nāṣir al-Uṭrūsh's testimony is insightful because he was similar in age to al-Ḥasan al-ʿAskarī and a contemporary of his. He reportedly witnessed the pertinent historical events that unfolded immediately after the death of al-Ḥasan al-ʿAskarī. See al-Naqḍ al-Muktafī of al-Naysābūrī (p. 66).

Furthermore, there were some early Shi'ite scholars who held that the alleged Mahdī was born as believed by the Twelvers, only to later die whilst in occultation, ending his imamate quite early in history. See Al-Fihrist of Ibn al-Nadīm (p. 219). Though much more can be said, all in all, the standard Twelver belief regarding the Mahdī was rejected and detested by many different schools of the Shia, let alone mainstream Islam.

Those who assert the existence of al-ʿAskarī's son maintain that he was two or more years old when his father passed away in 260. They maintain that he has been concealed since that time and that he has been Allah's proof (*ḥujja*) in the land since then: one's faith (*īmān*) cannot be considered complete without belief in him. They also claim that he is the Mahdī prophesized by the Messenger of Allah ﷺ and that he possesses comprehensive knowledge of everything lacking in the faith.

This is an area where the Muslim must exercise caution and scrupulousness, and he must seek guidance and assistance from Allah. Allah has prohibited speaking without proper knowledge, and He mentioned that this behavior is among the ways of the Shayṭān. And Allah has forbidden beliefs that conflict with the Truth, and this is attested to by the texts found in Revelation. Allah has also forbidden the following one's own whims (*al-hawā*).

Concerning the Mahdī foretold by the Prophet, the scholars specialized in the Prophet's traditions who have retained them and studied them alongside their transmitters – such as Abū Dāwūd, al-Tirmidhī and others – have reported information about him. Imām Aḥmed also reported about him in his *Musnad.*

It was reported from ʿAbdullāh ibn Masʿūd that he said, "The Messenger of Allah ﷺ said, 'If only one day remained in this world, Allah would prolong that day until He sends forth a man from my household, one who shares my name and whose father's name is the same as my father's name. He will fill the earth with justice and benevolence, just as it had once been filled with evil and tyranny.'"(1)

(1) Sunan Abī Dāwūd (6/337), al-Jāmiʿ al-Kabīr of al-Tirmidhī (4/75)

وقال من أثبته: إن أباه لما توفي سنة ستين ومئتين كان عمره سنتين أو أكثر من ذلك بقليل، وأنه غاب من ذلك الوقت، وأنه من ذلك الوقت حجة الله على أهل الأرض، لا يَتِمُّ الإيمانُ إلا به، وأنه هو المهدي الذي أخبر به النبي ﷺ، وأنه يَعلم كل ما يُفتَقر إليه في الدين.

وهذا موضع ينبغي للمسلم أن يَتثبَّتَ فيه ويَستهديَ الله ويستعينَه، فإن الله قد حرَّمَ القولَ بغير علم، وذكر أن ذلك من خُطوات الشيطان، وحَرَّم القولَ المخالفَ للحق، ونصوص التنزيل شاهدة بذلك، ونَهى عن اتباع الهوى.

فأما المهديّ الذي بَشَّرَ به النبي ﷺ فقد رواه أهل العلم العالمون بأخبار النبي ﷺ، الحافظونَ لها الباحثون عنها وعن رُواتِها، مثل أبي داود والترمذي وغيرهما. ورواه الإمام أحمد في "مسنده."

فعن عبد الله بن مسعود قال: قال رسول الله ﷺ: "لو لم يَبقَ من الدنيا إلا يومٌ لطَوَّل اللهُ ذلك اليومَ، حتى يَبعثَ الله فيه رجلا من أهل بيتي يُواطِئ اسمُه اسمي، واسمُ أبيه اسمَ أبي، يملأ الأرض قِسطًا وعدلاً كما مُلِئَتْ ظلمًا وجورًا."

This notion has also been reported Um Salama and others.(1) It was also reported from ʿAlī ibn Abī Ṭālib that he said, "The Mahdī is from the descendants of this son of mine," and he pointed to al-Ḥasan.(2) The Prophet ﷺ also said, "There shall be a caliph at the end of times who shall distribute wealth in handfuls."(3) This is an authentic ḥadīth.

The Prophet has mentioned that his name will be Muḥammad son of ʿAbdillāh, not Muḥammad son of al-Ḥasan. Those who consequently argued that Muḥammad ibn al-Ḥasan's forefather, al-Ḥusayn, had the *kunya*, "Abū ʿAbdillāh," have conflated the *kunya* with his name.(4) It is apparent to anyone who is fearful of Allah that this is a manipulation of the text away from its true context and that is akin to the esoteric interpretations of the Qarmatians.(5)

---

(1) Sunan Abī Dāwūd (6/341)
(2) Sunan Abī Dāwūd (6/347)
(3) Ṣaḥīḥ Muslim (4/2234-2235)
(4) This is a reference to some attempts by some Shi'ite apologists who desperately seek to reconcile the obvious contradiction between the reliable Prophetic tradition and their belief in the alleged Mahdī, who is Muḥammad son of al-Ḥasan. Since the reliable Prophetic tradition mentions that the Mahdī's father shall be named ʿAbdullāh, these Shi'ite polemicists have resorted to claiming that al-Ḥusayn, this Mahdī's distant forefather, had the nickname (*kunya*) of "Abū ʿAbdillāh." The desperate polemicist effectively is attempting to argue that the alleged Mahdī's ninth forefather having the nickname, "Abū ʿAbdillāh," is equivalent to the Prophet's statement, "His father's name is the same as my father's name."

This plea not only misrepresents the prophetic tradition at hand, but it also is a form of meddling in basic language, where speech is distorted and misrepresented in an attempt to make it subservient to Twelver Shi'ite dogma.
(5) In this context, the Qarmatians is a reference to a bundle of heretical movements within Islam that manipulated the Quran by distorting basic language. They were able to circumvent the overt teachings and rulings of Islam by dubiously claiming that scripture has an apparent exoteric meaning and a hidden esoteric meaning that is not visible to the masses.

ورُوِي هذا المعنى من حديث أم سلمة وغيره. وعن علي بن أبي طالب ﵁ أنه قال: "المهدي من ولد ابني هذا"، وأشار إلى الحسن. وقال ﷺ: "يكون في آخر الزمان خليفةٌ يَحثُو المالَ حَثْوًا." وهو حديث صحيح.

فقد أخبر النبي ﷺ أن اسمه "محمد بن عبد الله"، ليس "محمد بن الحسن." ومن قال: إن أبا جدِّه الحسين، وإن كنيةَ الحسينِ "أبو عبد الله"، فقد جعل الكنيةَ اسمَه. فما يَخفى على من يَخشى الله أن هذا تحريف الكلم عن مواضعه، وأنه من جنس تأويلات القرامطة.

Furthermore, the statement of the Commander of the Faithful (ʿAlī) clearly states that the Mahdī descends from al-Ḥasan, rather than al-Ḥusayn. In several ways, al-Ḥasan and al-Ḥusayn are analogous to Ishmael and Isaac, though al-Ḥasan and al-Ḥusayn were not prophets. This is why the Messenger of Allah ﷺ used to say to them, "I seek protection for you in the perfect words of Allah from every devil and beast, and from every evil eye," and he would then say, "Abraham used to pray for the protection Ishmael and Isaac with these words."(1)

Ishmael was the older and wiser of them, and that is why the Prophet ﷺ said while on the pulpit delivering a sermon with al-Ḥasan to his side, "This son of mine is a leader (*sayyid*), and through him, Allah will reconcile between two great factions of the Muslims."(2)

In the same way that the majority of prophets descended from Isaac, most of the noble *imāms* descended from al-Ḥusayn. Likewise, just as the final prophet, whose message reached all corners of the world, descended from Ishmael, the Mahdī, the rightly guided caliph and the last of the caliphs, will descend from al-Ḥasan.

Also, according to the law of the Quran and *Sunnah*, a two year-old should be restricted in his autonomy and in the management of his own wealth until he reaches puberty and demonstrates maturity, for he is an orphan.(3) Allah has stated, "Test the orphans until they reach the age of marriage. If you find them to be mature enough, hand over their properties to them. [Quran 4:6]"

---

(1) Ṣaḥīḥ al-Bukhārī (4/147)

(2) Ṣaḥīḥ al-Bukhārī (3/186, 9/56)

(3) Some Shi'ite traditions claim that he was slightly older than that, albeit still a young child. Either way, Ibn Taymiyya's point here is a valid and pertinent objection that stands.

وقول أمير المؤمنين صريح في أنه حَسَني لا حُسَيني، لأن الحسن والحسين مُشبِهانِ من بعض الوجوه بإسماعيل وإسحاقَ – وإن لم يكونا نبيَّينِ، ولهذا كان النبي ﷺ يقول لهما: "أُعِيذُكما بكلماتِ الله التامَّة، من كلّ شيطانٍ وهامَّةٍ، ومن كلِّ عينٍ لامَّة"، ويقول: "إن إبراهيم كان يُعوِّذ بهما إسماعيلَ وإسحاقَ."

وكان إسماعيل هو الأكبر والأحلم، ولهذا قال النبي ﷺ وهو يخطب على المنبر والحسنُ معه على المنبر: "إن ابني هذا سيّد، وسيُصلح الله به بين فئتين عظيمتينِ من المسلمين."

فكما أن غالبَ الأنبياء كانوا من ذرية إسحاق، فهكذا كان غالب السادة الأئمة من ذرية الحسين. وكما أن خاتم الأنبياء الذي طبَّق أمرُه مشارقَ الأرض ومغاربَها كان من ذرية إسماعيل، فكذلك الخليفة الراشد المهدي الذي هو آخر الخلفاء يكون من ذرية الحسن.

وأيضًا فإن من كان ابنَ سنتينِ كان في حكم الكتابِ والسنةِ مستحقًا أن يُحجَر عليه في بدنِه ويُحجَر عليه في مالِه حتى يَبلُغَ ويُؤنَسَ منه الرُّشدُ، فإنه يتيم. وقد قال الله تعالى: ﴿وَابْتَلُوا الْيَتَامَى حَتَّى إِذَا بَلَغُوا النِّكَاحَ فَإِنْ آنَسْتُمْ مِنْهُمْ رُشْداً فَادْفَعُوا إِلَيْهِمْ أَمْوَالَهُمْ﴾.

How could someone who is not permitted by the *Sharīʿa* to have autonomy over his own matters be entrusted with the *Ummah's* affairs? How can an individual who is unseen and unheard of be the leader over the *Ummah*? This is with the consideration that Allah does not command his slaves to obey someone inaccessible, yet the supposed Mahdī has been absent for 440 years![1] He is awaited by those who anticipate him, yet he has not emerged, for he does not exist.

Why does he not reveal himself to his close companions and loyalists, as his fathers did? What justifies this extraordinary concealment that was not observed by his predecessors?[2] Historically and in present times, the rational-minded would ridicule anyone who affirms such claims and bases his faith upon them, to the extent that the heretics (*zanādiqa*) utilize this belief and others like it as a tool to disparage the religion and undermine the intellects of the faithful for believing in such things.

The people of knowledge have thus uncovered many of the heretical *munāfiqīn* who conceal their disbelief by publicly professing such beliefs. They do so in an attempt to sway the hearts and minds of the weak and the people of whims in their direction. Because of that, much corruption has been introduced [into the faith] that Allah knows. There is no power nor strength except by Allah (*lā ḥawla wa-lā quwwata illā bi-llāh*). May Allah rectify the affairs of this *Ummah* and guide them!

---

(1) Given that the alleged Mahdī of Twelver Shi'ites supposedly went into occultation in the year 260 A.H, it may be inferred from this statement that Ibn Taymiyya wrote this treatise around the year 700 A.H, when he was around 39 years old. May Allah bestow His mercy upon him.

(2) These are reasonable questions that the sincere and careful observer who considers jeopardizing his faith with such odd and unfounded beliefs must first genuinely take into consideration. It should also be noted that Twelver Shi'ite apologists do posit "answers" to these questions, though they tend to be *ad hoc* and inconsistent in nature. The mere fact that an answer is provided by the apologist does not necessitate that it is a sufficient or acceptable solution that absolves the Shi'ite from the questions' original implications.

فمن لم تُفَوِّض الشريعةُ إليه أمرَ نفسه كيف تُفوِّضُ إليه أمرَ الأمة؟ وكيف يجوز أن يكون إمامًا على الأمَة من لا يُرى ولا يُسمَع له خبر؟ مع أنّ الله لا يُكلِّف العبادَ بطاعةِ من لا يَقدرون على الوصولِ إليه، وله أربعمئه وأربعون سنةً ينتظره من ينتظره وهو لم يخرج، إذ لا وجودَ له.

وكيف لم يظهر لخواصّه وأصحابِه المأمونين عليه كما ظهر آباؤه؟ وما المُوجِب لهذا الاختفاء الشديد دون غيرِه من الآباء؟ وما زال العقلاءُ قديمًا وحديثًا يضحكون ممن يُثبت هذا ويُعلِّق دينَه به، حتى جعلَ الزنادقةُ هذا وأمثالَه طريقًا إلى القَدحِ في الملَّة وتسفيهِ عقولِ أهلِ الدين إذا كانوا يعتقدون مثلَ هذا.

لهذا قد اطلع أهلُ المعرفة على خلقٍ كثيرٍ منافقينَ زنادقةٍ يتستَّرون بإظهار هذا وأمثالِه ليستميلوا قلوبَ وعقولَ الضعفاءِ وأهلِ الأهواء. ودَخلَ بسبب ذلك من الفساد ما الله به عليم، ولا حولَ ولا قوةَ إلا بالله العلي العظيم. والله يُصلح أمرَ هذه الأمة ويهديهم ويُرشِدهم.

[How Tomb Shrines Violate Islamic Fundamentals]

Likewise is what is relating to oaths, mosques and shrines [in the document]. Allah, in His Book and through His Prophet's *Sunnah*, which has been passed down by the forerunners and the successors from his family and others, has prescribed the building of mosques and the observance of prayers within them to the best of one's ability. He also prohibited the construction of mosques over graves, and he cursed those who did so.

Allah said, "The only people to maintain Allah's mosques are those who believe in Allah and the Last Day, and pray regularly, and give charity, and fear none but God. These are worthy of being from the guided. [Quran 9:18]"

Allah also said, "Who is more unjust than one who forbids the remembrance of God's name in places of worship and strives to have them ruined? These ought not to enter them except in fear. For them is disgrace in this world, and for them is a terrible punishment in the Hereafter. [Quran 2:115]"

Allah also said, "In houses which Allah has permitted to be built and have His name remembered therein. He is glorified therein at morning and evening by men who are neither distracted by trade nor commerce from remembrance of Allah, performance of prayers, and giving alms. [Quran 24:36-37]" Allah also said, "The places of worship are for God. So do not call anyone else alongside Allah. [Quran 72:18]" Allah also said, "Mosques—where the name of Allah is mentioned much. [Quran 22:40]"

وكذلك ما يتعلق بالنذور والمساجد والمشاهد، فإن الله في كتابه وسنة نبيه التي نقلها السابقون والتابعون من أهل بيته وغيرهِم قد أمرَ بعمارةِ المساجد وإقامة الصلواتِ فيها بحسب الإمكان، ونهى عن بناء المساجد على القبور، ولَعَن من يفعل ذلك.

قال الله تعالى: (إِنَّمَا يَعْمُرُ مَسَاجِدَ اللَّهِ مَنْ آمَنَ بِاللَّهِ وَالْيَوْمِ الْآخِرِ وَأَقَامَ الصَّلَاةَ وَآتَى الزَّكَاةَ وَلَمْ يَخْشَ إِلَّا اللَّهَ فَعَسَى أُولَئِكَ أَنْ يَكُونُوا مِنَ الْمُهْتَدِينَ).

وقال تعالى: (وَمَنْ أَظْلَمُ مِمَّنْ مَنَعَ مَسَاجِدَ اللَّهِ أَنْ يُذْكَرَ فِيهَا اسْمُهُ وَسَعَى فِي خَرَابِهَا أُولَئِكَ مَا كَانَ لَهُمْ أَنْ يَدْخُلُوهَا إِلَّا خَائِفِينَ).

وقال تعالى: (فِي بُيُوتٍ أَذِنَ اللَّهُ أَنْ تُرْفَعَ وَيُذْكَرَ فِيهَا اسْمُهُ يُسَبِّحُ لَهُ فِيهَا بِالْغُدُوِّ وَالْآصَالِ). وقال: (وَأَنَّ الْمَسَاجِدَ لِلَّهِ فَلَا تَدْعُو مَعَ اللَّهِ أَحَداً). وقال: (وَمَسَاجِدُ يُذْكَرُ فِيهَا اسْمُ اللَّهِ كَثِيراً).

The Prophet ﷺ said, "Whoever constructs a mosque for the sake of Allah, then Allah shall build a house for him in Paradise."(1) He also said, "Give good news to those who walk in the darkness of the night to the mosques, for they will have complete light on the Day of Resurrection."(2) The Prophet ﷺ also said, "Whoever goes to a mosque at dawn or dusk, then Allah shall prepare an abode for him [in Paradise] each time he goes."(3) The Prophet ﷺ also said, "A man's prayer in the mosque is twenty-five times better than his prayer at home or in his place of business."(4)

The Prophet ﷺ also said, "Whoever cleanses himself thoroughly at home and then goes to the mosque solely for the purpose of prayer will have one good dead and one bad deed forgiven with every two steps taken."(5) He also said, "A man's prayer with another man is better than his prayer alone. His prayer with two other men is better than his prayer with just man. Anything beyond that is even more beloved to Allah."(6)

The Prophet ﷺ also said, "There will be rulers over you who postpone the prayer beyond its appointed time. Therefore, perform the prayer at its proper time. Then, have your prayer with them be a voluntary prayer."(7) He ﷺ also said, "They pray for you. If they do well, it is for your benefit. If they do poorly, then it is for your benefit and their harm."(8) This is a very vast topic.

---

(1) Al-Jāmiʿ al-Kabīr of al-Tirmidhī (1/420), Ṣaḥīḥ Ibn Khuzayma (2/268)
(2) Ṣaḥīḥ Ibn Khuzayma (2/377), al-Mustadrak ʿalā al-Ṣaḥīḥayn (1/331)
(3) Ṣaḥīḥ al-Bukhārī (1/133), Ṣaḥīḥ Muslim (1/463)
(4) Ṣaḥīḥ al-Bukhārī (1/103), Ṣaḥīḥ Muslim (1/459)
(5) Ṣaḥīḥ Muslim (1/453)
(6) Musnad Aḥmed ibn Ḥanbal (35/189), Ṣaḥīḥ Ibn Ḥibbān (1/162)
(7) Ṣaḥīḥ Muslim (1/378)
(8) Ṣaḥīḥ al-Bukhārī (1/140)

وقال النبي ﷺ: "من بنى لله مسجدًا بنى الله له بيتا في الجنة." وقال: "بَشِّرِ المشَّائين في ظُلَمِ الليل إلى المساجد بالنور التامّ يومَ القيامة." وقال: "من غدا إلى المسجد أو راحَ، أعدَّ الله له نزلاً كلَّما غدا أو راح." وقال: "صلاةُ الرجل في المسجد تَفضُل على صلاتِه في بيته وسُوقِهِ بخمسٍ وعشرين درجةً."

وقال: "من تَطَهَّر في بيته فأحسنَ الطهورَ، وخرجَ إلى المسجد لا يُنهِزُه إلا الصلاةُ، كانتْ خطوتاه إحداهما تَرفعُ درجةً والأخرى تَضَعُ خطيئةً." وقال: "صلاةُ الرجل مع الرجل أزكى من صلاتِه وحدَه، وصلاتُه مع الرجلين أزكى من صلاتِه مع الرجل، وما كان أكثر كان أحبَّ إلى الله."

وقال: "سيكون عليكم أمراءُ يُؤخِّرون الصلاةَ عن وقتها، فصَلُّوا الصلاةَ لوقتها، ثمَّ اجعلوا صلاتكم معهم نافلةً." وقال: "يصلون لكم، فإن أحسنوا فلكم، وإن أساءوا فلكم وعليهم." وهذا باب واسعٌ جدًّا.

The Prophet ﷺ also said, "May Allah curse the Jews, for they have turned their prophets' graves into places of worship,"(1) warning against following in their footsteps. They said that had it not been for this, his grave would have been elevated; however, it is disliked that his grave be taken as a place of worship. The Prophet ﷺ expressed this during his illness. He also said five days prior to his death, "Those who came before you used to make graves into places of worship. Do not turn graves into places of worship. I forbid you from doing so."(2)

When the Messenger of Allah ﷺ mentioned the cathedral in Abyssinia, he said, "When a person among them dies, they construct a place of worship atop his grave and place those icons inside. They are the worse of creation in the eyes of Allah on the Day of Resurrection."(3) All of these ḥadīths are authentic and well-known.

The Messenger of Allah ﷺ also said, "May Allah curse the women who frequently visit graves and those who build places of worship on graves and adorn them with lights." Al-Tirmidhī and others reported this ḥadīth, and he said, "This ḥadīth is *ḥasan.*"(4)

If the Messenger of Allah ﷺ himself cursed those who construct places of worship on graves and adorn them with lights, how could a Muslim consider such actions as acts of worship and a means of closeness to Allah?

In *Ṣaḥīḥ Muslim*, it is reported that the Commander of the Faithful ʿAlī ibn Abī Ṭālib (may Allah be pleased with him) said, "The Messenger of Allah sent me with a mission, and he instructed me to not leave any elevated grave unlevelled nor any icon unerased."(5)

---

(1) Ṣaḥīḥ al-Bukhārī (2/88), Ṣaḥīḥ Muslim (1/376)
(2) Ṣaḥīḥ Muslim (1/377)
(3) Ṣaḥīḥ al-Bukhārī (1/93), Ṣaḥīḥ Muslim (1/375)
(4) Al-Jāmiʿ al-Kabīr of al-Tirmidhī (1/422), Ṣaḥīḥ Ibn Ḥibbān (3/107)
(5) Ṣaḥīḥ Muslim (2/666-667)

وقال أيضا: "لعنَ الله اليهودَ اتخذوا قبورَ أنبيائهم مساجدَ"، يُحذِّر ما فعلوا. قالوا: ولولا ذلك لأُبْرِزَ قبرُه، ولكن كُرِهَ أن يُتَّخذَ مسجدًا، وهذا قاله في مرضه . وقال قبل موته بخمسٍ: "إن من كان قبلكم كانوا يتخذون القبورَ مساجدَ، ألا فلا تتخذوا القبور مساجد، فإني أنهاكم عن ذلك."

ولما ذكر كنيسة الحبشة قال: "أولئك إذا مات الرجلُ فيهم بَنَوا على قبرِه مسجدًا وصَوَّروا فيه تلك التصاوير، أولئك شِرارُ الخلق عند الله يوم القيامة." وكل هذه الأحاديث في الصحاح المشاهير.

وقال أيضًا: "لعنَ الله زوَّاراتِ القبور والمتخذين عليها المساجَد والسُّرُجَ." رواه الترمذي وغيره، وقال: "حديث حسن."

فإذا كان النبي ﷺ قد لعن الذين يتخذون على القبورِ المساجدَ ويسرجون عليها الضوءَ، فكيف يَستحِلُّ مسلم أن يَجعلَ هذا طاعةً وقربةً؟

وفي صحيح مسلم عن أمير المؤمنين علي بن أبي طالب رضي الله عنه قال: "بَعثَنِي رسولُ الله ﷺ فأمرَني أن لا أدعَ قبرًا مُشْرِفًا إلا سوَّيتُه، ولا تِمثالاً إلا طَمستُه."

It has also been established from the Prophet ﷺ that he said, "O Allah, do not let my grave become an idol that is worshipped."(1) Additionally, he said, "Do not turn my grave into a site of ritual celebration. Pray for me wherever you are, as your prayers will reach me."(2) The Messenger of Allah ﷺ thus prohibited the ritual congregation around his grave, and he commanded that prayer be done for him in all places.

These ḥadīths were transmitted by the family of the Prophet, such as ʿAlī ibn al-Ḥusayn, from his father, from his grandfather;(3) as well as ʿAbdullāh ibn al-Ḥasan ibn ʿAlī ibn Abī Ṭālib. (4) They, alongside their neighbors from the scholars of Medīna, used to forbid innovated practices at the Prophet's grave and other burial sites out of adherence to his command and commitment to his *Sharīʿa.*

The practice of lingering around graves and icons of prophets and the righteous is a fundamental aspect of idolatry, even though idolatry did manifest through other means as well. In His Book, Allah quotes the polytheists saying, "'Do not abandon your gods. Do not forsake Wadd, Suwāʿ, Yaghūth, Yaʿūq, or Nasr.' They have led many astray. [Quran 71:23-24]" A group from the scholars from the predecessors (*Salaf*) reported that these deities were once righteous individuals. Upon their death, people gathered around their graves and eventually created icons in their honor.

Ibn ʿAbbās similarly commented on Allah's statement, "Have you considered al-Lāt and al-ʿUzzā? And Manāt, the third one, the other? [Quran 53:19-20]" Ibn ʿAbbās explained that al-Lāt was a man who used to prepare porridge for the pilgrims. After his death, people used to gather around his grave."(5)

---

(1) Al-Muwaṭṭaʾ – Riwāyat Yaḥyā al-Laythī (1/243)
(2) Muṣannaf ʿAbdirrazzāq (3/576).
(3) Muṣannaf Ibn Abī Shayba (5/177)
(4) Ibn Taymiyya may actually be referring to ʿAbdullāh's brother, al-Ḥasan ibn al-Ḥasan ibn ʿAlī ibn Abī Ṭālib. Refer to footnote #2.
(5) Tafsīr al-Ṭabarī (22/47), Ṣaḥīḥ al-Bukhārī (6/141)

وثبت عن النبي ﷺ أنه قال: "اللَّهُمَّ لا تجعلْ قبري وثنًا يُعبَد." وقال: "لا تتخذوا قبري عيدًا، وصَلُّوا عَليَّ حيثُما كنتم، فإنّ صلاتكم تبلغني." فنهى النبي ﷺ عن الاجتماع عند قبرِه، وأمرَ بالصلاة عليه في جميع المواضع، فإن الصلاةَ عليه تَصِل إليه من جميع المواضع.

وهذه الأحاديث رواها أهل بيته، مثلُ علي بن الحسين عن أبيه عن جدّه علي، ومثل عبد الله بن الحسن بن علي بن أبي طالب. فكانوا هم وجيرانُهم من علماء أهل المدينة يَنهون عن البدع التي عند قبرِه أو قبرِ غيرِه، امتثالاً لأمرِه متابعة لشريعتِه.

فإن من مبدأ عبادة الأوثان: العكوف على قبور الأنبياء والصالحين والعكوف على تماثيلهم، وإن كانت وقعت بغير ذلك. وقد ذكر الله في كتابه عن المشركين أنهم قالوا (لا تَذَرُنَّ آلِهَتَكُمْ وَلا تَذَرُنَّ وَدّاً وَلا سُوَاعاً وَلا يَغُوثَ وَيَعُوقَ وَنَسْراً وَقَدْ أَضَلُّوا كَثِيرًا). وقد روى طائفة من علماءِ السلف أن هؤلاء كانوا قومًا صالحين، فلمّا ماتوا عكفوا على قبورهم، ثمَّ صوَّروا تماثيلَهم.

وكذلك قال ابن عباس في قوله (أَفَرَأَيْتُمُ اللَّاتَ وَالْعُزَّى وَمَنَاةَ الثَّالِثَةَ الْأُخْرَى)، قال ابن عباس: "كان اللات رجلاً يَلُتُّ السويقَ للحجاج، فلما ماتَ عكفوا على قبرِه."

This is the reason the Prophet ﷺ said, "O Allah, do not let my grave become an idol that is worshipped,"[1] and forbade prayer at his grave. Consequently, when the Muslims integrated the Prophet's quarter into the mosque, they adjusted its edge's orientation and sealed it to prevent anyone from praying in the direction of the Prophet. That is because the Prophet ﷺ said, "Do not sit upon graves, and do not pray towards them." Muslim reported this ḥadīth.[2]

When the Prophet ﷺ used to visit the deceased at the Baqīʿ cemetery, he would greet them and supplicate for them. He taught his companions to recite the following words when visiting graves, "Peace be upon you, inhabitants of an abode of believers. God-willing, we shall follow in your footsteps. May Allah bestow His mercy upon those who have passed away before us among you and those yet to come. We ask Allah to bestow wellness upon us and you. O Allah, [...] their reward, and do not lead us astray after them, and forgive us and them."[3]

It is to be noted that buried within the Baqīʿ cemetery are the Prophet's son, Ibrāhīm, and his daughters, Um Kulthūm, Ruqayya, and Fāṭima, the mistress of all women. One of his daughters was buried therein early on, around the time of the Battle of Badr. Despite that, none of these disapproved innovations occurred at these nobles' gravesites. Instead, the prescribed practice is that greetings and supplications be offered for them by praying for their forgiveness (*istighfār*) and other forms.

(1) Al-Muwaṭṭa' – Riwāyat Yaḥyā al-Laythī (1/243)
(2) Ṣaḥīḥ Muslim (2/668)
(3) Ṣaḥīḥ Muslim (1/218, 2/669-671), Musnad Aḥmed ibn Ḥanbal (40/486). The traditions quote the Messenger of Allah saying, "O Allah do not forbid us their reward, and do not lead us astray after them."

ولهذا قال النبي ﷺ: "اللَّهُمَّ لا تجعل قبري وثنًا يُعبَد"، ونهى أن يُصلَّى عند قبره. ولهذا لما بنى المسلمون حُجرتَه حرَّفوا مؤخرها وسنموه لئلا يُصلَّى إليه، فإنه ﷺ قال: "لا تجلسوا على القبور ولا تُصلُّوا إليها"، رواه مسلم.

وكان ﷺ إذا خرجَ إلى أهل البقيع يُسلِّم عليهم ويدعو لهم. وعلَّم أصحابَه أن يقولوا إذا زاروا القبور: "سلامٌ عليكم أهلَ دارِ قوم مؤمنين، وإنا إن شاء الله بكم لاحقون، ويرحم الله المستقدمين منكم والمستأخرين، نسأل الله لنا ولكم العافية، اللَّهُمَّ اجرهم[1] ولا تَفْتِنّا بعدهم، واغفر لنا ولهم."

هذا مع أنّ في البقيع إبراهيم وبناته أم كلثوم ورقيَّة وسيدة نساءِ العالمين فاطمة، وكانت إحداهن دُفِنَتْ فيه قديمًا قريبًا من غزوة بدر، ومع ذلك فلم يُحدِثْ على أولئك السادة شيئًا من هذه المنكرات، بل المشروع التحيةُ لهم والدعاء بالاستغفار وغيره.

---

(1) لعله قد سقط بعض الشيء من هذا النص، فإن عامة الأخبار المروية في هذا المعنى تجعل دعاءه ﷺ: "اللَّهُمَّ لا تحرمنا أجرهم." فلذا تركت الكلمة بلا ضبط، والله أعلم وبالله التوفيق.

Similarly, in regards to the Messenger of Allah ﷺ, he instructed that prayers be offered for him both near and far. He said, "Offer abundant prayers for me on Fridays and Friday nights, as your prayers are brought before me." The people thus asked, "How can our prayers reach you once you have passed away?" He replied, "Allah has forbidden the land from consuming the bodies of the prophets."(1) The Prophet ﷺ also said, "Whenever a person passes by the grave of someone he knew in the *Dunyā* and offers a greeting, Allah sends the deceased's soul back to him, enabling him to respond to the greeting."(2)

All of these ḥadīths are authentic according to the specialists in the Prophet's ḥadīths. Supplications and prayers for forgiveness reach the deceased person whether offered at his grave or elsewhere. *Duʿāʾ* on the behalf of the deceased Muslims is how a Muslim should treat them, just as he would make *duʿāʾ* for them throughout his life.

Thus is the Messenger of Allah ﷺ who has commanded us to offer prayers and extend greetings to him and his family, both during his lifetime and after his passing. He also commanded us to pray for believing men and women while they are alive and dead, and at their graves as well as other locations.

Allah has forbidden us from taking equals to Him or equating the houses of the creation, which are their graves, with His own house, which is the Kaʿba and the Holy Sanctuary. Allah mandated that we undertake pilgrimage to His house, direct our prayers towards it, and circumambulate around it. Additionally, He prescribed that we receive its corners and kiss the Black Stone, which Allah has likened to His own right hand. Ibn ʿAbbās said, "The Black Stone is Allah's right hand on Earth. When one touches it and holds it by his hand, it is as though they have shaken hands with Allah and kissed Allah's right hand."(3)

---

(1) Ṣaḥīḥ Ibn Khuzayma (3/118), Ṣaḥīḥ Ibn Ḥibbān (1/353)
(2) This one ḥadīth is weak. See al-Dhahabī's Siyar Aʿlām al-Nubalāʾ (12/590).
(3) Muṣannaf ʿAbdirrazzāq (5/38)

وكذلك في حقّه أمر بالصلاة والسلام عليه من القرب والبعد، وقال: "أكثِروا عليَّ من الصلاة يوم الجمعة وليلةَ الجمعة، فإن صلاتكم معروضة عليَّ." قالوا: "كيف تُعرَض صلاتُنا عليك وقد أَرِمْتَ؟" يعني بَلِيْتَ. قال: "إنّ الله حرَّم على الأرض أن تأكلَ أجسادَ الأنبياء." وقال: "ما من رجلٍ يمرُّ بقبر الرجل كان يَعرفُه في الدنيا فيُسلِّم عليه إلا ردَّ الله عليه روحَه حتى يَرُدَّ عليه السلامَ."

وكلُّ هذه الأحاديث ثابتة عند أهل المعرفة بحديث النبي ﷺ. فالدعاء والاستغفار يصل إلى الميت عند قبرِه وغيرِ قبرِه، وهو الذي ينبغي للمسلم أن يعاملَ به موتى المسلمين، من الدعاء لهم بأنواع الدعاء، كما كان في حياته يدعو لهم.

وهذا رسولُ الله ﷺ قد أمرنا أن نصلِّيَ عليه ونُسلِّم تسليمًا في حياتِه ومماتِه، وعلى آل بيتِه، وأمَرنا أن ندعو للمؤمنين والمؤمنات في محياهم ومماتهم عند قبورهم وغير قبورِهم.

ونهانا الله أن نجعل له أندادًا، أو نُشبِّه بيتَ المخلوق الذي هو قبرُه ببيتِ الله الذي هو الكعبةُ البيت الحرامُ، فإنّ الله أمرنا أن نحجّ ونُصلّي إليه ونطوفَ به، وشرعَ لنا أن نَستلم أركانَه، ونُقبِّلَ الحجرَ الأسودَ الذي جعلَه الله بمنزلة يمينه. قال ابن عباس: "الحجر الأسود يمينُ الله في الأرض، فمن استلَمه وصافحَه فكأنما صافحَ الله وقَبَّلَ يمينَه."

Allah also decreed that the Kaʿba be adorned with drapery and curtains. Those who cling to its curtains can be likened to someone grasping another person's trailing garment, seeking refuge and protection. It is impermissible to equate the houses of the creation with Allah's house.(1) It is for this reason that the *Salaf* used to prohibit the visitors of the Prophet's grave from kissing it. Rather, they prescribed that one should greet him (May my parents be his ransom) and offer prayers on his behalf, just as the predecessors used to do.

The *Salaf*, who were more knowledgeable in Allah's religion, the *Sunnah* of His Prophet, the Prophet's rights, and the rights of the predecessors and successors from *Ahlulbayt* and beyond, refrained from engaging in any of these innovated practices that resemble idolatry and polytheism. That is because Allah and His Messenger prohibited them from doing such. Instead, they worshipped Allah alone, without any partners, devoting their faith to Him, as mandated by Allah and His Messenger.

They maintained the houses of Allah through their hearts and limbs in prayer, recitation of the Quran, engagement in *Dhikr*, supplication (*duʿāʾ*) and other acts. Given this, how could it be permissible for a Muslim to deviate from the Book of Allah, the *Sharīʿa* of His Prophet, and the path of the faithful forerunners, in favor of innovated practices introduced by other people, whether intentionally or in error?

---

(1) This section on Ibn Taymiyya should be quite profound to the careful observer. He acutely recognizes that many tomb shrines constructed later in Islamic history effectively functioned as alternate Kaʿbas in the minds of the heretics who excessively venerated them. Thus, it is not uncommon to witness many of the Shi'ite heretics rubbing graves and tombs, circumambulating around them, grasping onto them and beseeching them for aid, just as a Muslim would do when worshipping Allah at his holy sanctuary in Mecca.

It appears that the extremist Shi'ite heretics and forgers of the past were cognizant of this reality as well, which incited them to forge traditions that deemed Karbalāʾ, the site where al-Ḥusayn was martyred and subsequently buried, superior to the Kaʿba itself! See, as an example, the preposterous Twelver fabrications found in Kāmil al-Ziyārāt of Ibn Qūlawayh (p. 489-496).

وشرعَ كسوةَ الكعبةِ وتعليقَ الأستارِ عليها، وكان يتعلَّق من يتعلَّق بأستار الكعبة كالمتعلق بأذيال المستجار به، فلا يجوز أن تُضاهَى بيوتُ المخلوقين ببيت الخالق. ولهذا كان السلف ينهون من زَارَ قبرَ النبي ﷺ أن يُقبِّلَه، بل يُسلِّم عليه -بأبي هو وأمي ﷺ ويُصلِّي عليه، كما كان السلف يفعلون.

فإذا كان السلفُ أعرفَ بدين الله وسنةِ نبيه وحقوقِه، وحقوقِ السابقين والتابعين من أهل البيت وغيرِهم، ولم يفعلوا شيئًا من هذه البدع التي تُشبِه الشركَ وعبادةَ الأوثان، لأن الله ورسوله نهاهم عن ذلك، بل يعبدون الله وحده لا شريك له، مخلصين له الدينَ كما أمر الله به ورسولُه.

ويَعْمُرون بيوتَ الله بقلوبهم وجَوارِحِهم من الصلاةِ والقراءةِ والذكرِ والدعاء وغير ذلك؛ فكيفَ يَحِلُّ للمسلم أن يَعدِلَ عن كتاب الله وشريعةِ رسوله وسبيلِ السابقين من المؤمنين، إلى ما أحدثَه ناسٌ آخرون، إمَّا عمدًا وإمَّا خطأً؟

The carrier of this letter has been informed that it is impermissible for a Muslim to support these innovated practices which conflict with the Quran and the *Sunnah* (*bidaʿ*) that are upon the graves of prophets, nobles of *Ahlulbayt*, and the *sheikhs*. This is all with the assumption that these graves are authentic in the first place. Given that most of these alleged graves are actually disputed, what then would the ruling [of these innovations be]?!

If these oaths sworn in devotion to the graves are indeed a sin prohibited by Allah, His Messenger and the faithful forerunners, then the Messenger of Allah ﷺ has said, "Whoever has sworn an oath to obey Allah, then they should execute it. Whoever has sworn an oath to disobey Allah, then they should not disobey Him."(1) This ḥadīth is in the authentic collections.

Thus, if the oath is an act of obedience to Allah and His Messenger, such as a person swearing an oath of prayer, fasting, pilgrimage (*ḥajj*), charity, and similar things, then he should execute it.

However, if the oath involves an act of disobedience, whether it constitutes disbelief or not, such as an oath devoted to idols like the *Budūd*(2) in India or what the polytheists [of Arabia] used to make to their idols – such as al-Lāt in al-Ṭāʾif, al-ʿUzzā in ʿArafa near Mecca, and Manāt the Third for the people of Medīna – then it should not be executed. These three cities are the cities of Hejaz. The polytheists used to swear oaths in devotion to these idols, perform religious rituals in worship of them, and beseech them as intermediaries between themselves and Allah for their needs. As Allah quoted them saying, "We only worship them so that they bring us nearer to God. [Quran 39:3]"

---

(1) Ṣaḥīḥ al-Bukhārī (8/142)

(2) *Budūd* is a loanword in Arabic that refers to idols. I would like to thank Sheikh Nabeel Nisar Sheikh for bringing this reading of the text to my attention, and I would also like to thank Sheikh Joe Bradford for further confirming this reading of the text with an example. See Masālik al-Abṣār of al-ʿUmarī (3/74).

فخُوطِب حاملُ هذا الكتاب بأن جميعَ هذه البدع التي على قبورِ الأنبياء والسادة من آل البيت وَالمشايخ، المخالفة للكتاب والسنة، ليس للمسلم أن يُعِين عليها هذا إذا كانت القبورُ صحيحةً، فكيف وأكثرُ هذه القبور مطعونٌ فيها؟

وإذا كانت هذه النذورُ للقبور معصيةً قد نهى الله عنها ورسولُه والمؤمنون السابقون، فقد قال النبي ﷺ: "مَن نَذَرَ أن يطيعَ اللهَ فليُطِعْه، ومن نَذَر أن يَعصِيَ الله فلا يَعْصِه." وقال ﷺ: "كفارة النذر كفارة يمين"، وهذا الحديث في الصحاح.

فإذا كان النذرُ طاعةً لله ورسوله، مثل أن ينذرَ صلاةً أو صومًا أو حجًّا أو صدقةً أو نحو ذلك، فهذا عليه أن يَفِيَ به.

وإذا كان النذرُ معصيةً -كفرًا أو غيرَ كفرٍ- مثل أن ينذر للأصنام كالنذور [كالبدود] التي بالهند، ومثلما كان المشركون ينذرون لآلهتهم، مثل اللات التي كانت بالطائف، والعُزَّى التي كانت بعرفةَ قريبًا من مكة، ومناة الثالثة الأخرى التي كانت لأهل المدينة. وهذه المدائن الثلاث هي مدائن أرض الحجاز، كانوا ينذرون لها النذور ويتعبدون لها ويتوسَّلون بها إلى الله في حوائجهم، كما أخبر الله عنهم بقوله: (مَا نَعْبُدُهُمْ إِلَّا لِيُقَرِّبُونَا إِلَى اللَّهِ زُلْفَى).

Similarly, [if the oath involves an act of disobedience] like what the ignorant among Muslims swear in devotion to springs of water, wells, water canals, stones, trees, or graves – even if it is the grave of a prophet or righteous person – or if they swear to provide oil, wax, draperies or silver to some of these objects, then these are all oaths of disobedience that should not be executed.

Nonetheless, some scholars have stated that a person who makes such an oath must offer the penalty for breaking an oath as compensation. This view is based on what the authors of the *Sunan* reported from the Prophet ﷺ that he said, "There shall be no oath in an act of disobedience, and its penalty is that of breaking an oath."(1)

If any wealth or possessions initially devoted to these impermissible practices are later redirected towards a prescribed good deed, then that is good. For example, the oil would be used to light the houses of Allah; or the money and drapery would be given to deserving Muslims from the family of the Messenger of Allah ﷺ and the rest of the believers; and these resources would be allocated to the rest of the public goods mandated by Allah and His Messenger.

Any ignorant person who believes that these forbidden oaths have actually lead to the fulfillment of their own needs by providing wealth, health and other similar benefits, or by warding off harm from an adversary and the like, is mistaken in that belief. It has been authentically reported from the Prophet ﷺ that he discouraged such oaths, saying, "They do not bring any good; instead, they draw out goodness from the miserly."(2)

(1) Sunan Abī Dāwūd (5/182), al-Jāmiʿ al-Kabīr of al-Tirmidhī (3/155), Sunan Ibn Mājah (3/257-258), al-Mujtabā of al-Nasāʾī (7/26)

(2) Ṣaḥīḥ Muslim (3/1261), Ṣaḥīḥ al-Bukhārī (8/124)

ومثلما ينذر الجهَّالُ من المسلمين لعينِ ماءٍ أو بئرٍ من الآبار أو قناةِ ماءٍ أو مغارةٍ أو حجرٍ أو شجرةٍ من الأشجار أو قبرٍ من القبور – وإن كان قبرَ نبي أو رجلٍ صالح – أو ينذرون زيتًا أو شمعًا أو كسوةً أو ذهبًا أو فضةً لبعضِ هذه الأشياء، فإن هذا كلَّه نذر معصيةٍ لا يُوفَى به.

لكن من العلماء من يقول: على صاحبه كفارةُ يمين، لما روى أهلُ السنن عن النبي ﷺ: "لا نذرَ في معصيةٍ، وكفارتُه كفارةُ يمينٍ". وفي الصحيح عنه أنه قال: "كفارة النذرِ كفارةُ يمين."

وإذا صُرِفَ من ذلك المنذور شيءٌ في قُربةٍ من القُرُباتِ المشروعة كان حسنًا، مثلَ أن يَصرِف الدُّهنَ إلى تنويرِ بيوتِ الله، ويَصرِف المالَ والكسوةَ إلى من يَستحقّه من المسلمين من آل بيتِ رسولِ الله ﷺ، وسائرِ المؤمنين، وفي سائر المصالحِ التي أمر الله بها ورسولُه.

وإذا اعتقدَ بعضُ الجهَّال أن بعضَ هذه النذور المحرَّمة قد قَضَتْ حاجتَه بجَلْبِ المنفعةِ مِنِ المال والعافية ونحو ذلك، أو بدَفْع المضرَّة من العدو ونحوه، فقد غَلِط في ذلك. فقد صحَّ عن النبي ﷺ أنه نهى عن النذر وقال: "إنه لا يأتي بخيرٍ، ولكنّه يُستَخرجُ به من البخيل."

The Messenger of Allah ﷺ thus considered oaths unfavorable, even though their execution is mandatory when the oath pertains to an act of obedience to Allah and His Messenger. The Messenger of Allah ﷺ has also stated that oaths do not bring good; rather, they draw out goodness from a miserly person. This notion has been authentically reported from the Messenger of Allah ﷺ through several routes about oaths that purely are acts of obedience to Allah. Considering this, what would the verdict be regarding an oath that embodies polytheism (*shirk*)? Such an oath is neither permissible to swear nor to execute.

Although Islam has faded and ritual gatherings around the graves of the righteous from *Ahlulbayt* and others have surged, it is imperative for the people to obey Allah and His Messenger. They must adhere to Allah's religion, which Allah sent His prophet, and they must refrain from legislating things into faith that were not authorized by Allah. The purpose of Allah sending prophets and revealing books [to them] is to ensure that the entirety of religion belongs solely to Allah and that people worship Allah alone, without any partners.

It is as Allah said, "Inquire Our messengers whom We sent before you, 'Did We designate gods besides the Most Gracious to be worshiped?' [Quran 43:45]" Moreover, Allah said, "He prescribed for you the same religion He enjoined upon Noah, and what We inspired to you, and what We enjoined upon Abraham, Moses, and Jesus, 'Uphold the religion, and do not be divided within it.' As for the idolaters, the call you extend to them is outrageous to them. Allah chooses for Himself whom He wills, and He guides to Him those who repent. [Quran 42:13]"

Allah also said, "To every community We sent a messenger [with the message], 'Worship God, and shun idolatry.' Allah guided some of them, while others were destined for misguidance. Journey through the earth and observe the fate of those who denied the truth. [Quran 16:36]"

فعدَّ النذر مكروهًا، وإن كان الوفاءُ به واجبًا إن كان المنذور طاعةً لله ورسوله ﷺ.وقد أخبرَ النبي ﷺ أن النذرَ لا يأتي بخير، وإنما يُستَخرج به من البخيل. وهذا المعنى قد ثبت عن النبي ﷺ من غير وجهٍ فيما كان قُربةً محضةً لله، فكيف بنذر فيه شركٌ؟ فإنه لا يجوز نذرُه ولا الوفاءُ به.

وهذا وإن كان قد غمر الإسلام، وكَثُرَ العكوفُ على القبور التي هي للصالحين من أهلِ البيت وغيرِهم، فعَلَى الناس أن يُطيعوا الله ورسولَه، ويتبعوا دينَ الله الذي بَعثَ به نبيَّه ﷺ، ولا يَشرَعُوا من الدين ما لم يأذنْ به اللهُ، فإن الله إنما أرسلَ الرسلَ وأنزلَ الكتبَ ليكون الدينُ كلُّه لله، وليعبدوا الله وحدَه لا شريك له.

كما قال تعالى: (وَاسْأَلْ مَنْ أَرْسَلْنَا مِنْ قَبْلِكَ مِنْ رُسُلِنَا أَجَعَلْنَا مِنْ دُونِ الرَّحْمَنِ آلِهَةً يُعْبَدُونَ)، وقال تعالى: (شَرَعَ لَكُمْ مِنَ الدِّينِ مَا وَصَّى بِهِ نُوحاً وَالَّذِي أَوْحَيْنَا إِلَيْكَ وَمَا وَصَّيْنَا بِهِ إِبْرَاهِيمَ وَمُوسَى وَعِيسَى أَنْ أَقِيمُوا الدِّينَ وَلا تَتَفَرَّقُوا فِيهِ كَبُرَ عَلَى الْمُشْرِكِينَ مَا تَدْعُوهُمْ إِلَيْهِ اللَّهُ يَجْتَبِي إِلَيْهِ مَنْ يَشَاءُ وَيَهْدِي إِلَيْهِ مَنْ يُنِيبُ).

وقال تعالى: (وَلَقَدْ بَعَثْنَا فِي كُلِّ أُمَّةٍ رَسُولاً أَنِ اعْبُدُوا اللَّهَ وَاجْتَنِبُوا الطَّاغُوتَ فَمِنْهُمْ مَنْ هَدَى اللَّهُ وَمِنْهُمْ مَنْ حَقَّتْ عَلَيْهِ الضَّلالَةُ).

And Allah said about those who call upon angels and prophets [in worship], "Say, 'Call upon those you invoke besides Him. They possess no power to alleviate your hardships or alter them.' Those whom they invoke are themselves seeking proximity to their Lord, competing for closeness, hoping for His mercy, and fearing His punishment. Indeed, your Lord's punishment is to be feared. [Quran 17:56-57]"

And Allah said, "He would not instruct you to regard the angels and prophets as lords beside Allah. Would he command you to disbelieve after you have submitted? [Quran 3:80]"

Allah addressed those who seek intercessors other than Him, saying, "Or have they chosen intercessors besides God? Say, 'Even though they possess no power over anything and lack reason?' Say, 'All intercession belongs to Allah. To Him belongs dominion over the heavens and the earth. Then, to Him you shall return.' When Allah alone is invoked, the hearts of those who disbelieve in the Hereafter are repulsed. However, when others besides Him are invoked, they are filled with joy. Say, 'Our God, Creator of the heavens and the earth, Knower of all secrets and declarations: You will judge between your servants concerning their disagreements.' [Quran 39:43-46]"

Allah also said, "They have regarded their rabbis and priests as lords instead of Allah, as well as the Messiah son of Mary. Yet, they were commanded to worship none but One God. There is no god but He. Exalted is He beyond what they associate with hin. [Quran 9:31]"

Allah further said, "Who is he that can intercede with Allah except with His permission? [Quran 2:255]" Additionally, Allah said, "How many an angel is there in the heavens whose intercession is of no avail unless Allah grants permission to whomever He chooses and accepts. [Quran 53:26]" Allah also states, "They do not intercede except for those whom He approves. [Quran 21:28]" And Allah said, "Intercession holds no worth with Him, save for those He has permitted. [Quran 34:23]"

وقال تعالى في حق الذين كانوا يدعون الملائكةَ والنبيين: (قُلِ ادْعُوا الَّذِينَ زَعَمْتُمْ مِنْ دُونِهِ فَلا يَمْلِكُونَ كَشْفَ الضُّرِّ عَنْكُمْ وَلا تَحْوِيلاً أُولَئِكَ الَّذِينَ يَدْعُونَ يَبْتَغُونَ إِلَى رَبِّهِمُ الْوَسِيلَةَ أَيُّهُمْ أَقْرَبُ وَيَرْجُونَ رَحْمَتَهُ وَيَخَافُونَ عَذَابَهُ إِنَّ عَذَابَ رَبِّكَ كَانَ مَحْذُوراً).

وقال: (وَلا يَأْمُرَكُمْ أَنْ تَتَّخِذُوا الْمَلائِكَةَ وَالنَّبِيِّينَ أَرْبَاباً أَيَأْمُرُكُمْ بِالْكُفْرِ بَعْدَ إِذْ أَنْتُمْ مُسْلِمُونَ).

وردَّ على من اتخذ شفعاءَ من دونه فقال: (أَمِ اتَّخَذُوا مِنْ دُونِ اللَّهِ شُفَعَاءَ قُلْ أَوَلَوْ كَانُوا لا يَمْلِكُونَ شَيْئاً وَلا يَعْقِلُونَ قُلْ لِلَّهِ الشَّفَاعَةُ جَمِيعاً لَهُ مُلْكُ السَّمَاوَاتِ وَالْأَرْضِ ثُمَّ إِلَيْهِ تُرْجَعُونَ وَإِذَا ذُكِرَ اللَّهُ وَحْدَهُ اشْمَأَزَّتْ قُلُوبُ الَّذِينَ لا يُؤْمِنُونَ بِالْآخِرَةِ وَإِذَا ذُكِرَ الَّذِينَ مِنْ دُونِهِ إِذَا هُمْ يَسْتَبْشِرُونَ قُلِ اللَّهُمَّ فَاطِرَ السَّمَاوَاتِ وَالْأَرْضِ عَالِمَ الْغَيْبِ وَالشَّهَادَةِ أَنْتَ تَحْكُمُ بَيْنَ عِبَادِكَ فِي مَا كَانُوا فِيهِ يَخْتَلِفُونَ).

وقال: (اتَّخَذُوا أَحْبَارَهُمْ وَرُهْبَانَهُمْ أَرْبَاباً مِنْ دُونِ اللَّهِ وَالْمَسِيحَ ابْنَ مَرْيَمَ وَمَا أُمِرُوا إِلَّا لِيَعْبُدُوا إِلَهاً وَاحِداً لا إِلَهَ إِلَّا هُوَ سُبْحَانَهُ عَمَّا يُشْرِكُونَ)

وقال تعالى: (مَنْ ذَا الَّذِي يَشْفَعُ عِنْدَهُ إِلَّا بِإِذْنِهِ) وقال تعالى: (وَكَمْ مِنْ مَلَكٍ فِي السَّمَاوَاتِ لا تُغْنِي شَفَاعَتُهُمْ شَيْئاً إِلَّا مِنْ بَعْدِ أَنْ يَأْذَنَ اللَّهُ لِمَنْ يَشَاءُ وَيَرْضَى). وقال تعالى: (وَلا يَشْفَعُونَ إِلَّا لِمَنِ ارْتَضَى) وقال: (وَلا تَنْفَعُ الشَّفَاعَةُ عِنْدَهُ إِلَّا لِمَنْ أَذِنَ لَهُ).

Throughout the entirety of Allah's books, devotion of faith is consistently instructed to be solely toward Allah. This is especially the case with the Book that Muḥammad was sent with or the *Sharīʿa* that he brought, as it has perfected religion. Allah proclaimed, "Today, I have perfected your religion for you. [Quran 5:4]" Allah also said, "Then We set you on a path of faith, so adhere to it, and do not follow the whims of those who know not. [Quran 45:18]"

Devotion to Allah and justice in all affairs were deemed the backbone of faith, as Allah said, "Say, 'My Lord commands justice, and that you stand devoted in every place of worship. Thus, invoke Him and consecrate your faith solely to Him. As He initiated your existence, so shall you return.' Some He has guided, while others have deserved misguidance. [Quran 7:29-30]"

The Prophet ﷺ has refined the oneness of Allah (*tawḥīd*) from all subtle and overt manifestations of polytheism (*shirk*), even to the extent that he said, "Whoever swears by anything other than Allah has committed *shirk*." Al-Tirmidhī reported and authenticated this ḥadīth.(1)

---

(1) Al-Jāmiʿ al-Kabīr of al-Tirmidhī (3/162), Ṣaḥīḥ Ibn Ḥibbān (3/300)

This example and the examples that follow are a testimony to Ibn Taymiyya's profound deployment of scripture and ḥadīth to substantiate and explain his position. Here, he cites a host of authentic traditions where the Messenger of Allah, out of aversion to any resemblance of *shirk*, forbade practices that may seem benign and miniscule to many readers. The underlying point made by Ibn Taymiyya here is that such texts, barring all of the other evidences cited earlier in this letter, should exemplify the extreme measures the Messenger of Allah upheld to eradicate *shirk* and the veneration of other than Allah.

If merely swearing by the name of one's righteous ancestor is prohibited and akin to *shirk*, then one could only imagine how severe the Islamic verdict would be against prostrating to that ancestor's grave, circumambulating around it, beseeching it for aid, offering sacrifices to it and treating it like a house of Allah etc.

وكُتُبُ الله من أولها إلى آخرها تأمر بإخلاص الدين لله، لاسيما الكتاب الذي بُعِثَ به محمد ﷺ، أو الشريعة التي جاء بها، فإنها كملت الدين. قال تعالى: (الْيَوْمَ أَكْمَلْتُ لَكُمْ دِينَكُمْ)، وقال: (ثُمَّ جَعَلْنَاكَ عَلَى شَرِيعَةٍ مِنَ الْأَمْرِ فَاتَّبِعْهَا وَلَا تَتَّبِعْ أَهْوَاءَ الَّذِينَ لَا يَعْلَمُونَ).

وقد جعل قِوامَ الأمر بالإخلاص لله والعدلِ في الأمور كلها، كما قال تعالى: (قُلْ أَمَرَ رَبِّي بِالْقِسْطِ وَأَقِيمُوا وُجُوهَكُمْ عِنْدَ كُلِّ مَسْجِدٍ وَادْعُوهُ مُخْلِصِينَ لَهُ الدِّينَ كَمَا بَدَأَكُمْ تَعُودُونَ فَرِيقًا هَدَى وَفَرِيقًا حَقَّ عَلَيْهِمُ الضَّلَالَةُ).

ولقد خَلَّص للنبي ﷺ التوحيدَ من دقيقِ الشرك وجليلِه، حتى قال: "مَن حَلَفَ بغير الله فقد أشرك". رواه الترمذي وصححه.

The Prophet ﷺ also said, "Allah prohibits you from swearing by your fathers. If one must swear, let him either swear by Allah or remain silent."(1) This ḥadīth is well-known and in the authentic collections.

The Prophet ﷺ also said, "Do not say, 'What Allah and Muḥammad have willed.' Instead, say, 'What Allah willed, and then what Muḥammad subsequently willed'."(2)

Similarly, a man once addressed the Prophet, saying, "What Allah and yourself have willed." To this, the Prophet ﷺ responded, "Have you made me an equal to Allah?! Rather, say, 'What Allah alone has willed.'"(3)

It was also reported from the Prophet ﷺ that he said, "In this nation, *shirk* is more subtle than the creeping of ants."(4) It has also been reported from him that performing religious rituals to garner praise or admiration from people is *shirk*.(5)

And Allah said, "Whoever hopes to meet their Lord should perform righteous deeds and never associate anyone with the worship of their Lord. [Quran 18:110]" The Prophet ﷺ also taught some of his companions to say, "O Allah, I seek refuge in you from knowingly associating partners with you, and I seek forgiveness from you for that which I do unknowingly."(6)

---

(1) Ṣaḥīḥ al-Bukhārī (8/27, 8/132), Ṣaḥīḥ Muslim (3/1267)
(2) Musnad Aḥmed ibn Ḥanbal (38/364), Ṣaḥīḥ Ibn Ḥibbān (3/86)
(3) Musnad Aḥmed ibn Ḥanbal (3/339, 4/341, 5/297)
(4) Musnad Aḥmed ibn Ḥanbal (32/383)
(5) Sunan Ibn Mājah (5/126), al-Mustadrak ʿalā al-Ṣaḥīḥayn (1/44)
(6) Al-Adab al-Mufrad of al-Bukhārī (p. 328)

وقال ﷺ: "إن الله ينهاكم أن تحلفوا بآبائكم، فمن كان حالفًا فليحلف بالله أو ليصمت". وهذا مشهور في الصحاح.

وقال ﷺ: "لا يقولنَّ أحدُكم ما شاء الله وشاء محمد، ولكن قولوا ما شاء الله ثمَّ شاءَ محمد."

وقال له رجل: ما شاءَ الله وشِئتَ، فقال ﷺ: "أجَعلتَني لله نِدًّا؟! بل ما شاء اللهُ وحدَه."

ورُوِي عنه ﷺ أنه قال: "الشركُ في هذه الأمة أخفَى من دبيب النمل." ورُوِيَ عنه ﷺ أن الرياء شرك.

وقال تعالى: (فَمَنْ كَانَ يَرْجُوا لِقَاءَ رَبِّهِ فَلْيَعْمَلْ عَمَلاً صَالِحاً وَلا يُشْرِكْ بِعِبَادَةِ رَبِّهِ أَحَداً). وعَلَّمَ بعضَ أصحابه أن يقول: "اللَّهُمَّ إني أعوذ بك من أن أُشرِكَ بك وأنا أعلم، وأستغفرَك لما لا أعلم."

Pertinent to this notion are those who request or give charity for reasons other than Allah's sake, such as those who say, "[This charity is] for such-and-such person's sake," be it a person from the *Ṣaḥāba* or *Ahlulbayt*. The collection of charity in their names thus becomes a means to unfairly consume the people's wealth. Consequently, some people who ascribe themselves to the love of *Ahlulbayt* end up donating to some of them, and others who ascribe themselves to the *Sunnah* donate to others. However, the Shayṭān has taken hold of them all!

Charity and all other acts of worship are only prescribed to be done for the sake of Allah, as Allah said, "But the devout shall evade the Hellfire. He who gives his money to become pure, seeking no favor in return, but only seeking his Lord's acceptance, the Most High. And he will be made content. [Quran 92:17-21]"

Allah also said, "And what you give in charity, desiring Allah's approval, those individuals are the ones for whom reward is multiplied. [Quran 30:39]" And Allah said, "The parable of those who spend their wealth striving for Allah's approval and to fortify their souls is that of a garden on a hillside. When abundant rain falls upon it, its yield doubles. Even if no heavy rain falls, then dew is sufficient. [Quran 2:265]"

And Allah said, "In their love of Allah, they feed the poor, the orphan, and the captive, saying, 'We feed you solely for the sake of Allah. We expect neither recompense nor gratitude from you.' [Quran 76:8-9]"

Allah made a comprehensive statement, saying, "Those who received the Scripture did not splinter until the Clear Evidence was brought to them. They were instructed only to worship God, devoting their faith exclusively to Him, observe regular prayer, and to offer alms. That is the upright religion. [Quran 98:5]" Worship of Allah encompasses prayer and all that it embodies, such as supplication and *dhikr*, as well as charity and *zakat* of all forms, including food, clothing, money and other items.

ومن هذا الباب الذين يسألون الصدقةَ أو يُعطُونها لغير الله، مثل من يقول: لأجلِ فلان – إما بعض الصحابة أو بعض أهل البيت، حتى يتخذَ السؤالَ بذلك ذريعةً إلى أكل أموالِ الناس بالباطل، ويَصير قومٌ ممن يَنتسِبُ إلى محبة آل البيت يُعطِي الناسَ، وآخرون ممن ينتسب إلى السنة يُعطِي الآخرين، والشيطانُ قد استحوذَ على الجميع.

فإن الصدقة وسائر العبادات لا يُشْرَعُ أن تُفْعَلَ إلا لله، كما قال تعالى: ﴿وَسَيُجَنَّبُهَا الْأَتْقَى الَّذِي يُؤْتِي مَالَهُ يَتَزَكَّى وَمَا لِأَحَدٍ عِنْدَهُ مِنْ نِعْمَةٍ تُجْزَى إِلَّا ابْتِغَاءَ وَجْهِ رَبِّهِ الْأَعْلَى وَلَسَوْفَ يَرْضَى﴾.

وقال تعالى: ﴿وَمَا آتَيْتُمْ مِنْ زَكَاةٍ تُرِيدُونَ وَجْهَ اللَّهِ فَأُولَئِكَ هُمُ الْمُضْعِفُونَ﴾. وقال: ﴿وَمَثَلُ الَّذِينَ يُنْفِقُونَ أَمْوَالَهُمُ ابْتِغَاءَ مَرْضَاتِ اللَّهِ وَتَثْبِيتاً مِنْ أَنْفُسِهِمْ كَمَثَلِ جَنَّةٍ بِرَبْوَةٍ أَصَابَهَا وَابِلٌ فَآتَتْ أُكُلَهَا ضِعْفَيْنِ فَإِنْ لَمْ يُصِبْهَا وَابِلٌ فَطَلٌّ﴾.

وقال: ﴿وَيُطْعِمُونَ الطَّعَامَ عَلَى حُبِّهِ مِسْكِيناً وَيَتِيماً وَأَسِيراً، إِنَّمَا نُطْعِمُكُمْ لِوَجْهِ اللَّهِ لا نُرِيدُ مِنْكُمْ جَزَاءً وَلا شُكُوراً﴾.

وقال تعالى كلمة جامعة: ﴿وَمَا تَفَرَّقَ الَّذِينَ أُوتُوا الْكِتَابَ إِلَّا مِنْ بَعْدِ مَا جَاءَتْهُمُ الْبَيِّنَةُ وَمَا أُمِرُوا إِلَّا لِيَعْبُدُوا اللَّهَ مُخْلِصِينَ لَهُ الدِّينَ حُنَفَاءَ وَيُقِيمُوا الصَّلاةَ وَيُؤْتُوا الزَّكَاةَ وَذَلِكَ دِينُ الْقَيِّمَةِ﴾. وعبادتُه تَجمعُ الصلاةَ وما يَدخُل فيها من الدعاء والذكر، وتَجمع الصدقةَ والزكاةَ بجميع الأنواع من الطعام واللباس والنقد وغير ذلك.

May Allah make us and the rest of our faithful brethren devoted to Him in faith, worshipping him alone without associating anything with Him, clinging to His rope, adhering to His Book, and learning the revelations of Scripture and Wisdom. May Allah protect us from the devils of mankind and *jinn*, granting us refuge from their attempts to divert us from His path. May He guide us to the straight path, the path of the prophets, the sincere, the martyrs, and the righteous. Indeed, excellent are those as companions!

All praise is due to Allah, Lord of all creation. May Allah bestow blessings and abundant salutations upon Muḥammad and his family.[1]

---

[1] I completed this text's translation on the 17th of Shawwāl, 1444 A.H. (5/7/2023). May the blessings of Allah be upon Prophet Muḥammad, his companions, his household and all believers who strive to follow them in righteousness and sincerity. *Āmīn.*

May Allah also bestow His mercy upon the author of this treatise, *Sheikh al-Islām* Taqī al-Dīn Ibn Taymiyya, and may Allah cool his grave and englighten it with blessings and illuminations until the day we are all resurrected from our graves. *Āmīn.* And all praise is due to Allah, Lord of all creation.

والله يجعلنا وسائرَ إخواننا المؤمنين مخلصين له الدين، نعبده ولا نشرك به شيئًا، معتصمين بحبله، متمسكين بكتابه، متعلمين لما أنزل من الكتاب والحكمة، ويَصرِف عنّا شياطينَ الجن والإنس، ويُعِيذُنا أن تفرّق بنا عن سبيله، ويهدينا الصراطَ المستقيم، صراط الذين أنعم عليهم من النبيين والصديقين والشهداء والصالحين، وحَسُنَ أولئك رفيقا.

والحمد لله رب العالمين، وصلى الله على محمد وآله وسلّم تسليمًا كثيرًا.

تمّت ترجمة هذه الرسالة إلى اللغة الإنجليزية يوم الأحد السابع عشر من شوال سنة 1444 من الهجرة، على صاحبها أفضل الصلاة والسلام إلى يوم الدين.

وكتب مترجمها عبد الله بن محمد الرّبّاط حامدًا مُصلّيًا مُسَلِّمًا.

Bibliography

Al-Aṣbaḥī, Mālik ibn Anas, *Muwaṭṭa' Mālik – Riwāyat Yaḥyā al-Laythī*, Bashār ʿAwwād Maʿrūf, ed., 2nd ed., (Beirut, 1417/1997).

Al-Bazzār, Aḥmed b. ʿAmr, *Musnad al-Bazzār*, Maḥfūẓ Al-Raḥmān Zaynallah et al., eds., 1st ed., (Medina, 1988-2009).

Al-Buhūtī, Manṣūr ibn Yūnus, *al-Rawḍ al-Murbiʿ Sharḥ Zād al-Mustaqniʿ*, Turkī ibn Saʿūd Al-Dhiyābī, ed., 1st ed., (Dammam, 1440).

Al-Bukhārī, Muḥammad ibn Ismāʿīl, *al-Adab al-Mufrad*, ʿAlī Mazīd and ʿAlī Riḍwān, eds., 1st ed., (Cairo, 1422).

——. *Ṣaḥīḥ al-Bukhārī*, Muḥammad Zuhayr Al-Nāṣir, ed., 1st ed., (Beirut, 1423).

Al-Dhahabī, Muḥammad ibn Aḥmed, *Siyar Aʿlām al-Nubalā'*, Shuʿayb Al-Arnā'ūṭ et al., eds., 3rd ed., (Damascus, 1405/1985).

Al-Dārimī, Abdullāh ibn ʿAbdirraḥmān, *Musnad al-Dārimī*, Ḥusayn Al-Dārānī, ed., 1st ed., (Riyadh, 1412).

Al-Ḥāzimī, Ibrāhīm ibn ʿAbdillāh, *Mawsūʿat Aʿlām al-Qarn al-Rābiʿ ʿAshar wal-Khāmis ʿAshar*, 1st ed., (Riyadh, 1419).

Ibn Abī Shayba, Abū Bakr ʿAbdullāh, *al-Muṣannaf*, Muḥammad ʿAwwāma, ed., 1st ed., (Beirut, 1427/2006).

Ibn Abī Yaʿlā, Muḥammad, *Ṭabaqāt al-Ḥanābila*, Muḥammad Al-Faqī, ed., Cairo, n.d.

Ibn Bābawayh, Muḥammad ibn ʿAlī, *ʿIlal al-Sharā'iʿ*, 1st ed., (Beirut, 1427/2006).

Ibn Ḥajar, ʿAḥmed ibn ʿAlī, *al-Maṭālib al-ʿĀliya bi-Zawā'id al-Masānīd al-Thamāniya*, Saad Al-Shithti, ed., 1st ed., (Riyadh, 1419).

Ibn Ḥanbal, Aḥmed ibn Muḥammad, *Musnad al-Imām Aḥmed Ibn Ḥanbal*, Shuʿayb Al-Arnāʾūṭ et al., eds., 1st ed., (Beirut, 1421/2001).

Ibn Ḥibbān, Muḥammad, *Ṣaḥīḥ Ibn Ḥibbān*, Muḥammad ʿAlī Sonmez and Khāliṣ Aydemīr, eds., 1st ed., (Beirut, 1433).

Ibn Hishām, ʿAbdulMalik ibn Hishām, *al-Sīra al-Nabawayiyya*, Muṣtafā al-Saqqā et al, eds., 2nd ed., (Cairo, 1375).

Ibn al-Jawzī, ʿAbdurraḥmān ibn ʿAlī, *Kitāb al-Mawḍūʿāt*, ʿAbdurraḥmān ʿUthmān, ed., 1st ed., (Medina, 1386).

Ibn Khuzayma, Muḥammad ibn Isḥāq, *Ṣaḥīḥ Ibn Khuzayma*, Muḥammad Muṣṭafā al-Aʿẓamī, ed., (Beirut, 1400).

Ibn Mājah, Muḥammad ibn Yazīd, *Sunan Ibn Mājah*, Shuʿayb Al-Arnāʾūṭ et al, eds. 1st ed., (Damascus , 1430).

Ibn al-Nadīm, Muḥamamd ibn Isḥāq, *al-Fihrist*, Ibrāhīm Ramaḍān, ed., 2nd ed., (Beirut, 1417/1997).

Ibn al-Qayyim, Muḥammad ibn Abī Bakr, *Madārij al-Sālikīn Bayna Manāzili Iyyāka Naʿbudu wa-Iyyāka Nastaʿīn*, Muḥammad Al-Baghdādī, ed., 3rd ed., (Beirut, 1416/1996).

Ibn Qūlawayh, Jaʿfar ibn Muḥammad, *Kāmil al-Ziyārāt*, Muḥammad Zakī Al-Jaʿfarī, ed., 1st ed., (Qom, 1435).

Ibn Rajab, ʿAbdurraḥmān ibn Aḥmed, *Dhayl Ṭabaqāt al-Ḥanābila*, ʿAbdurraḥmān al-ʿUthaymīn, ed., 1st ed., (Riyadh, 1425/2005).

Ibn Saʿd, Muḥammad, *al-Ṭabaqāt al-Kabīr*, ʿAlī Muḥammad ʿUmar, ed., 1st ed., (Cairo, 1421/2001).

Ibn Taymiyya, Aḥmed ibn ʿAbdilḤalīm, *Jāmiʿ al-Masāʾil*, Muḥammad Ozair Shams, ed., 1st ed., (Mecca, 1422).

——. *Ḥuqūq Āl al-Bayt*, ʿAbdulQādir ʿAṭā, ed., 2nd ed., (Beirut, 1407/1987).

——. *Minhāj al-Sunna al-Nabawiyya fī Naqḍ Kalām al-Shīʿa wa-l-Qadariyya*, Muḥammad Sālim, ed., 1st ed., (Riyadh, 1406/1986).

Al-ʿImrān, ʿAlī, and Muḥammad Shams, *al-Jāmiʿ li-Sīrat Shaykh al-Islām Ibn Taymiyya Khilāl Sabʿat Qurūn*, 2nd ed., (Mecca, 1422).

Al-Naysābūrī, al-Ḥākim Muḥammad ibn ʿAbdillāh, *al-Mustadrak ʿalā al-Ṣaḥīḥayn*, Muṣṭafā ʿAbdulqādir ʿAṭā, ed., 1st ed., (Beirut, 1411/1990).

Al-Naysābūrī, Muḥammad ibn Aḥmed, *al-Naqḍ al-Muktafī ʿalā Man Yaqūlū bi-l-Imām al-Mukhtafī*, Al-Kazem Al-Zaydi, ed., 1st ed., 1422/2021.

Al-Naysābūrī, Muslim b. al-Ḥajjāj, *Ṣaḥīḥ Muslim*, Muḥammad Fuʾād ʿAbdilBāqī, ed., 1st ed., (Cairo, 1412/1991).

Al-Nasāʾī, Aḥmed ibn Shuʿayb, *al-Mujtabā min al-Sunan*, ʿAbdulFattāḥ Abū Ghuddah, ed., 2nd ed., (Aleppo, 1406/1986).

Al-Rabbat, Abdullah, *Schisms of the Shia: A Series of Illustrations*, 1st ed., (Coppel, 2022).

Al-Samʿānī, ʿAbdulkarīm ibn Muḥammad, *Kitāb al-Ansāb*, ʿAbdurraḥmān ibn Yaḥyā Al-Muʿallimī et al., eds., 1st ed., (Hyderabad, 1382).

Al-Ṣanʿānī, ʿAbdurrazzāq b. Hammām, *al-Muṣannaf*, Ḥabīb Al-Raḥmān Al-ʿAẓmī, ed., 2nd ed., (Beirut, 1403).

——. *Tafsīr ʿAbdirrazzāq*, Maḥmūd ʿAbdo, ed., 1st ed., (Beirut, 1419).

Al-Shāfiʿī, Muḥammad ibn Idrīs, *al-Musnad*, Beirut, 1400.

Al-Ṣijistānī, Sulaymān ibn al-Ashʿath, *Sunan Abī Dāwūd*, Shuʿayb Al-Arnāʾūṭ and Muḥammad Kāmil, eds., 1st ed., (Damascus, 1430).

Al-Ṭabarī, Muḥammad ibn Jarīr, *Tafsīr al-Ṭabarī*, ʿAbdullāh Al-Turkī, ed., 1st ed., 1422.

Al-Thaqafī, Muḥammad b. ʿĀṣim, *Juzʾ Muḥammad ibn ʿĀṣim al-Thaqafī*, Mufīd Khālid ʿĪd, ed., 1st ed., (Riyadh, 1409).

Al-Tirmidhī, Muḥammad b. ʿĪsā, *al-Jāmiʿ al-Kabīr*, Bashār ʿAwwād Maʿrūf, ed., Beirut, 1998.

Al-ʿUlaymī, ʿAbdurraḥmān ibn Muḥammad, *al-Manhaj al-Aḥmad fī Tarājim Aṣḥāb al-Imām Aḥmad*, ʿAbdulQādir al-Arnāʾūṭ and Ḥasan Marwa, eds., 1st ed., (Beirut, 1997).

Al-ʿUmarī, Aḥmed ibn Yaḥyā ibn Faḍlillāh, *Masālik al-Abṣār fī Mamālik al-Amṣār*, 1st ed., (Abu Dhabi, 1423).

www.ingramcontent.com/pod-product-compliance
Lightning Source LLC
LaVergne TN
LVHW022011080426
835513LV00009B/680